ADAM HAMILTON

Author of *Creed, The Walk,* and *The Journey*

PREPARE THE WAY
FOR THE LORD

ADVENT
AND THE MESSAGE OF JOHN THE BAPTIST

Abingdon Press | Nashville

To LaVon,
on our fortieth wedding anniversary.
I love you so very much and
am deeply grateful for your friendship,
partnership, and love.

CONTENTS

INTRODUCTION

In those days John the Baptist appeared in the desert of Judea announcing, "Change your hearts and lives! Here comes the kingdom of heaven!" He was the one of whom Isaiah the prophet spoke when he said:

The voice of one shouting in the wilderness,
> "Prepare the way for the Lord;
> make his paths straight."

Matthew 3:1-3

"Hurry!" LaVon shouted, as I was searching for the keys to my car. Contractions were getting closer, and it was time to head to the hospital. We'd spent months preparing for the birth of our daughter. We'd decorated the nursery, assembled a crib and changing table, and, with the help of friends and family, gathered diapers, clothes, and everything else she could possibly need. We'd also spent months preparing ourselves emotionally, praying and reading about how to be a parent. As the pregnancy progressed, excitement, anticipation, and not a little anxiety filled the air. Once at the hospital, we had more contractions for LaVon and more waiting for us both. And while the waiting seemed interminable at times, our daughter was finally born, and our world was forever changed.[1]

The preparation, waiting, and anticipation of childbirth is an apt metaphor for the season of Advent. The word Advent comes from the Latin *adventus*, which means coming, arrival, or presence. Advent, the liturgical season, starts four Sundays before Christmas and can be as long as twenty-eight days and as short as twenty-two. If you could summarize the aim of Advent, it would be captured by the words of Isaiah, words that defined John the Baptist's work and mission: "Prepare the way of the Lord" (Isaiah 40:3; Matthew 3:3; Mark 1:3; Luke 3:4 NRSV).

We often think of Advent as a season to prepare to celebrate anew the birth of Jesus—his first advent—but it is more than that. Advent is also focused on preparing for Christ's return—his second advent—either at his Second Coming at the climax of human history, or when he returns for us at our death. The prayer in the United Methodist "Service of Death and Resurrection" captures the aim of Advent's focus as it relates to Christ's return:

Help us to live as those who are prepared to die.
And when our days here are accomplished,
> enable us to die as those who go forth to live,
> so that living or dying, our life may be in you,
> and that nothing in life or in death will be
> able to separate us from your great love in
> Christ Jesus our Lord.[2]

Advent calls us to prepare the way of the Lord in our lives and in our world.

Advent calls us to prepare the way of the Lord in our lives and in our world.

Jesus speaks on several occasions about his second advent. The letters of the New Testament mention his return again and again. As Jesus spoke of his second coming, he challenged his hearers with words like these: "You also must be ready, for the Son of Man is coming at an unexpected hour" (Matthew 24:44; Luke 12:40). In Matthew 25 he illustrates this point with the parable of the ten bridesmaids, the parable of the talents, and the parable of the sheep and the goats, all of which describe some who were found ready and some who were not when the bridegroom, the master, or the king returns. The consequences were tragic for those who were not prepared.

My life as a pastor is filled with constant reminders of just how suddenly and unexpectedly death can come for us. In the month I completed this manuscript, I sat with two different families whose young adult daughters died unexpectedly and another family whose father died unexpectedly. It is true, Advent is about rightly celebrating Christmas, but it is also about knowing that Christ will one day return and living in such a way that we are found ready on that day. Doing so allows us to live as people of hope.

Advent and John the Baptist

This book is a series of reflections on the life of John the Baptist and, for many, it will be an Advent study. What does John the Baptist have to do with Advent? And why are two of Advent's four Sundays dedicated to the telling of John's story, his ministry and his message? Because John's mission, like Advent's mission, was to "prepare the way of the Lord." No other figure in scripture is more closely associated with this idea of preparation, of making people ready for the coming of Christ, than John the Baptist.

A little history is helpful when seeing John's connection to Advent. In the ancient world, when rulers announced their plans to leave their capital to make official visits to other regions of their kingdom, the people prepared for their coming. Such visits were, in the Roman Empire, described as the *adventus* of the visiting ruler. This was particularly true of a visit from the emperor. There were *adventus* ceremonies to formally receive the emperor when he arrived and *adventus* celebrations in the capital when he returned. Notre Dame historian Sabine MacCormack described what is known from Hellenistic sources of these *adventus* events:

> When the arrival of a ruler in a city was announced ahead of time, the citizens would decorate their city, and on the appointed day, a procession of citizens, headed by their dignitaries, would go out to a certain point outside the city walls, where they would meet the ruler.... Those in the procession would carry flowers, olive or palm-branches, lights and incense... Singing and acclamations [ensued].[3]

This kind of welcome for a ruler was not original to the Romans. Most ancient cultures had such practices. MacCormack's description even helps us understand what was happening on Palm Sunday when Jesus entered Jerusalem. The Romans even, at times, minted coins to celebrate the arrival, or return, of the emperor. Below is an example of a coin from the time of Emperor Philip I, who reigned from AD 244–249. The emperor sits upon a horse, hand upraised, greeting the people. Above him are the words, *ADVENTUS AUGG*—Aug, short for Augustus, a title that here identified the rider with the emperor.

Roman coin showing Emperor Philip I. "ADVENTUS AUGG" appears above him in the image on the right.

Now, here's the point we cannot miss. Before the arrival of the emperor, pharaoh, king, or queen, often months ahead of time, *a messenger was sent to prepare the way* for the monarch's arrival, to make sure that the people and their leaders were ready for his or her coming. John the Baptist was that messenger sent by God to prepare the people for the arrival of the long-awaited messianic king. This is why each of the four Gospels begins with John the Baptist before turning to Jesus's public ministry. Matthew 3:1-3 records:

In those days John the Baptist appeared in the desert of Judea announcing, "Change your hearts and lives! [Repent!] Here comes the kingdom of heaven!" He was the one of whom Isaiah the prophet spoke when he said:

> The voice of one shouting in the wilderness,
>> "Prepare the way for the Lord;
>> make his paths straight."

John was sent by God to prepare the people for the coming of Christ. In this book we'll examine his life, ministry, and message so that we might, in our own lives, "prepare the way for the Lord."

Lord, as I begin this study of the life and ministry of John the Baptist, I pray that you will speak to me. Help me to know this remarkable prophet in ways I had not before. Help me to hear your word to me through John's story, his preaching and witness, so that I might appropriately celebrate your birth anew, and be prepared for the day I meet you face to face.

1

THE ANNUNCIATION: "GOD HAS HEARD YOUR PRAYERS"

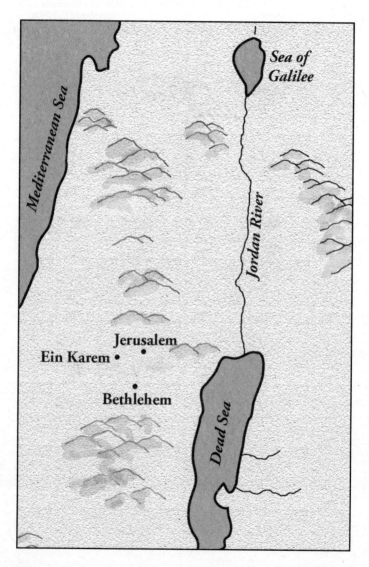

1

THE ANNUNCIATION: "GOD HAS HEARD YOUR PRAYERS"

I am sending my messenger, who will prepare the way before me.

Malachi 3:1 (NRSV)

During the rule of King Herod of Judea there was a priest named Zechariah who belonged to the priestly division of Abijah. His wife Elizabeth was a descendant of Aaron. They were both righteous before God, blameless in their observance of all the Lord's commandments and regulations. They had no children because Elizabeth was unable to become pregnant and they both were very old. One day Zechariah was serving as a priest before God because his priestly division was on duty. Following the customs of priestly service, he was chosen by lottery to go into the Lord's sanctuary and burn incense. All the people who gathered to worship were praying outside during this hour of incense offering. An angel from the Lord appeared to him, standing to the right of the altar of incense. When Zechariah saw the angel, he was startled and overcome with fear.

The angel said, "Don't be afraid, Zechariah. Your prayers have been heard. Your wife Elizabeth will give birth to your son and you must name him John."

Luke 1:5-13

We begin our study of the life and message of John the Baptist where his story begins in Luke's Gospel, with an older couple named Zechariah and Elizabeth.

The year was 5 BC. Herod the Great, with the support of the Romans, ruled as king over Judea. At 67, Herod had become increasingly paranoid, and his health was in decline. Many anticipated his death, and some hoped this was the time that God would raise up a king from the line of David, a king who would rule with righteousness and justice. Some wondered if this would be the time when the prophetic message of Zechariah, written a half a millennium earlier, might be fulfilled:

Rejoice greatly, Daughter Zion.
Sing aloud, Daughter Jerusalem.
Look, your king will come to you.
He is righteous and victorious.

He is humble and riding on an ass,
on a colt, the offspring of a donkey.
(Zechariah 9:9)

Zechariah, the father of John, likely named for that earlier prophet, was among those who hoped that a righteous and victorious ruler would soon come.

Zechariah was a priest of the division of Abijah. A thousand years earlier, according to 1 Chronicles, King David had divided the priests into twenty-four divisions. All of the divisions would serve together for the yearly festivals such as Passover, when Jerusalem's streets would be filled with crowds. In addition, each division would be assigned duties at the Temple two weeks out of the year. When not serving at the Temple, priests could live wherever they wished, and likely wherever they lived they served as something like a parish priest for their community, teaching, offering pastoral care, and praying for the sick. Elizabeth was a "descendent of Aaron," which likely means that she was, herself, the daughter of a priest.

Luke tells us that they lived in "a city in the Judean highlands" (Luke 1:39). Jerusalem is surrounded by hill country. While Luke provides no more detail, the tradition of the church is that they lived in a village today called Ein Karem, about four miles from Jerusalem's Temple. (See the map at the beginning of this chapter.) There are two

The traditional site of the birthplace of John the Baptist, in a grotto beneath The Church of Saint John the Baptist in Ein Karem.

well-known churches in Ein Karem that celebrate John the Baptist's story. One purports to be built atop the ancient well where Elizabeth would have drawn water. The other is built over a grotto said to be where John the Baptist was born. Whether or not this is Elizabeth and Zechariah's village, or whether these churches mark the actual places water was drawn and John was born, we cannot know. But the churches there beautifully help pilgrims remember the story of John's conception and birth.

With this as a backdrop, let's explore in more detail Luke's telling of the story of John's parents and the annunciation to them that they would conceive and bear a son whom they were to call John.

Elizabeth and Zechariah's Infertility

Luke begins the story of Elizabeth and Zechariah by writing, "They were both righteous before God, blameless in their observance of all the Lord's commandments and regulations. They had no children because Elizabeth was unable to become pregnant and they both were very old" (Luke 1:6-7). These two sentences summarize both a lifetime of faithfulness and a long journey of sorrow and disappointment.

While today, there are an increasing number of adults of childbearing age choosing not to have children,[1] this was not the case in the biblical world. In the ancient world, everyone was expected to have offspring. In addition to the emotional desire to have children, there was an economic importance as children assisted with work and, as parents grew older, adult children cared for their aging parents.

. But then, as today, there were couples who struggled with infertility. The Mayo Clinic reports that between 10 and 15 percent of couples who wish to conceive are unable to do so in any given year.[2] We don't know if the number was higher or lower in biblical times, but there are multiple couples in scripture, like Elizabeth and Zechariah, who went years without being able to have children.

In the biblical world, the physical causes of infertility were not understood, leaving many to believe that God was the one who opened or closed a woman's womb. At times in scripture, childlessness or barrenness were seen as punishments from God. Some Christians still believe that today—seeing their own infertility as God's will, or even God's punishment. But many do not see infertility this way.

Doctors have discovered dozens of physiological reasons why a woman might not be able to conceive, or why a man's sperm count might be too low to ensure conception. And researchers have found ways to treat infertility. I don't believe God afflicts women or men with the conditions that prevent conception or carrying a child to term, any more than I believe God makes his children sick with cancer or intentionally infects us with COVID-19.

Women and men in scripture, as today, felt deep disappointment, grief, and pain in infertility. I have been with many families over the years who knew this kind of pain, and often a profound disappointment with God, because of their inability to conceive. This is true even when we understand the underlying physiological factors involved in infertility.

For those who have struggled with infertility, notice Luke's description of Elizabeth and Zechariah: "They were both righteous before God, blameless in their observance of all the Lord's commandments and regulations." Their infertility was not because of sin. It was not because God did not love them or that God was displeased with them. Luke simply says that "Elizabeth was unable to become pregnant." It would appear that there was a physiological reason for Elizabeth's infertility, something affecting her or Zechariah, that kept them from having a child.

"Your Prayers Have Been Heard"

Luke continues:

One day Zechariah was serving as a priest before God because his priestly division was on duty. Following the customs of priestly service, he was chosen by lottery to go into the Lord's sanctuary and burn incense. All the people who gathered to worship were praying outside during this hour of incense offering.

(Luke 1:8-10)

As we learned above, each division of priests, in addition to serving during the festivals, was assigned two weeks out of the year to serve at the Temple performing a variety of functions. Still, it was only a handful of priests each day that were selected to enter the Holy Place, the sanctuary

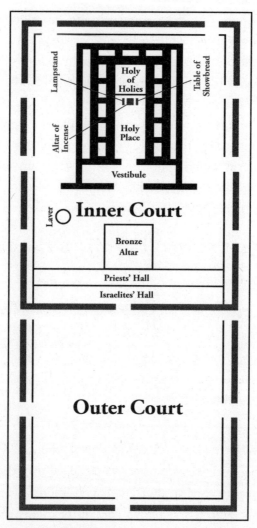

Diagram of the Temple

A scale model of the Temple and the city of Jerusalem.

of the Temple. With thousands of priests, the chance of entering the sanctuary to offer incense, bring in the bread offering, or fill the lampstands with oil might happen once in a priest's lifetime.

On this day, Zechariah was chosen to burn incense in the Temple. Shafts of light shown through the smoke of the incense from the clerestory windows high above the sanctuary floor. Oil lamps burned in the golden lampstand illuminating the beauty of this space. The walls were covered with carvings of winged creatures, palm trees, and blossoming flowers. Zechariah undoubtedly tried to take it

11

all in as he approached the gold altar on which he was to burn the incense. It sat just before the entrance to the Holy of Holies, God's throne room. Just then, Luke tells us, "An angel from the Lord appeared to him, standing to the right of the altar of incense. When Zechariah saw the angel, he was startled and overcome with fear" (Luke 1:11-12).

> Most of the angels we meet in scripture are not winged beings, but look like ordinary people.

The word *angel*, in Greek, literally means messenger, and most of the angels we meet in scripture are not winged beings, but look like ordinary people. This is why the writer of Hebrews tells his readers to welcome strangers because in so doing they may be welcoming angels without knowing it (Hebrews 13:2 NRSV). Nevertheless, Zechariah was overcome with fear and must have recognized this stranger was no mere mortal. But it was the words of Gabriel, not his appearance, that would leave Zechariah speechless. "The angel said, 'Don't be afraid, Zechariah. Your prayers have been heard. Your wife Elizabeth will give birth to your son and you must name him John'" (Luke 1:13).

Zechariah couldn't believe his ears. "Your prayers have been heard…Elizabeth will give birth to your son." Zechariah and Elizabeth had been married for decades. For years he must have prayed, again and again, that Elizabeth would conceive and bear a child. How many tears had been shed by Elizabeth when she had been unable to conceive? At their advanced age, it was likely Zechariah had stopped praying that prayer years before.

I wonder if there are things you have prayed for a long time, for years, but have seen no answer? I have recently begun seeing what looks like the answer to a prayer I've prayed almost daily for thirty-one years. At times I'd stopped praying about this, wondering if my prayers for it really mattered. On many occasions, I'd told the person I'd been praying for about my prayer for her. Recently she told me, "That prayer you've been praying for me—I didn't think what you'd prayed for was even possible. But now, I feel like the very thing you asked for is what I'm experiencing." Our prayers are always heard, even if we don't see the results we're looking for or they don't come in the time frame we hope.

When it comes to prayer, it is important to understand how prayer "works." Prayer is primarily about communion with God, giving thanks, offering praise, placing our life in God's hands, inviting God to lead and guide us, to forgive

13

us, and to use us. Prayer, like our conversations with friends or family, is not primarily about asking for things. It is not our effort to advise God on how to run the universe. And prayer is more about connecting with God and drawing strength, grace, and guidance from our faith, than it is about God solving all of our problems and removing all of our pain.

I've taught our congregation that it's okay to pray for the "grand-slam, out-of-the-park" kind of miracles. But it's important to recognize that God's primary way of working in our world is not to suspend the laws of nature to answer our prayers through miraculous intervention. We lay before God the desires of our hearts—health, healing, children, jobs, a mate—and we recognize that God's primary way of working is through the laws God has established, through the care of others, and through the strength and guidance God gives by the Spirit.

I was speaking with a woman recently whose husband was battling stage four cancer. One day he was fine, the next day he was in the hospital battling for his life. I loved how this woman articulated her faith. She said to me, "I don't see God as a genie in a bottle granting me three wishes. I prayed for healing, but I also prayed, 'God, we can't face this mountain without you. Please just hold my hand, that I can know you are with me, with us, and that you'll help us through this, whatever happens.'"

Several weeks later her husband died, but not before we gathered around his bedside to talk about faith, about God's love and grace, and about the significance of the resurrection of Christ. We spoke about Christ's promise to prepare a place for us and what heaven might be like. Then, with his wife and children holding his hands, touching him tenderly, I anointed his head with oil, and we committed his heart and life to Christ. His wife felt that Christ had taken her hand, and his hand, sustaining them and carrying them even through the "valley of the shadow of death."

If God's ordinary way of working was to produce miracles when people simply pray hard enough, or pray just the right words, or when enough people pray, we would not need doctors. No one would ever remain sick, be infertile, die young, lose their jobs, or have a bad day. We'd pray, and God would immediately fix things. That way of thinking about prayer, as my parishioner shared, makes God the genie in our bottle. But that is not what we find in scripture or in our lives. When we pray, we do so in relationship with God. We come in prayer to draw strength from God. We are not asking to be delivered from the realities of the human experience, but to invite God to walk with us as our companion, our deliverer, our Lord. I think of Thomas Dorsey's classic gospel prayer, "Precious Lord, take my hand, lead me on, let me stand…" or the well-known hymn, "What a friend we have in Jesus…" Both point to the power of God's presence with us in the midst of adversity or pain.

That's not to say that God cannot bring about the out-of-the-park-home-run miracles. I continue to pray for them, even as I understand they are not the norm. God is never offended by our honestly sharing our hopes and desires. And the story of John's conception is an example of God's miraculous intervention. But notice that this miracle occurs not when Zechariah and Elizabeth are in their twenties and praying so fervently for a child. It happens decades later, when God's unfolding plan *needs* a messenger to prepare the way for the Messiah. Yet, when God looked for a woman to bear this messenger, God remembered the prayers of Zechariah and Elizabeth and chose them for this important role in God's redemptive plans.

This theme of infertility and God's intervention at unexpected times in order to fulfill God's greater purposes shows up again and again in scripture. Sarah and Abraham struggled with infertility, but it wasn't until they were ninety and one hundred years old that they had their son, Isaac. Isaac and Rebekah were unable to conceive, but when Isaac was nearly sixty Rebekah had twins, Jacob and Esau. Jacob's wife Rachel could not conceive, but finally, after much grief, she conceived and gave birth to Joseph (of the *Amazing Technicolor Dreamcoat* fame!). There would be no Jewish people were it not for God's compassionate intervention in the lives of these couples.

Add to the patriarchs and matriarchs of Israel the story of Manoah and his wife who, again by a miracle, conceived and brought the great warrior Samson into this world. Then there is the story of Hannah and Elkanah in 1 Samuel and their conception of the prophet Samuel. Their story, and Hannah's faith, shaped Luke's telling of both Elizabeth's and Mary's stories in his Gospel. Though the author of 1 Samuel assumed God had shut Hannah's womb, he noted God's mercy in allowing Hannah to conceive after years of infertility. As a result, she dedicated her son, Samuel, to God and, from that time on, Samuel was raised by Eli the priest. We'll see in chapter 3 that something similar may have happened with John the Baptist. In 1 Samuel 2, Hannah sang a song of praise to God, a song that became the pattern for Mary's own Magnificat we'll study in chapter 2. And, like John the Baptist, Hannah and Elkanah's son, Samuel, became a great prophet of God.

These stories teach us that infertility was a real issue among God's people in the Bible, that there was pain for these families who struggled with it, that God heard their prayers but did not miraculously intervene at the time they prayed, and that God had compassion for those who struggled with infertility.

Thank God for
Unanswered Prayers?

I love Garth Brooks's song, "Unanswered Prayers." In it, the singer describes going to a hometown football game with his wife, only to run into his old high school flame. He remembers how, each night back in high school, he prayed that "God would make her mine." But as he reflected on his life since then, his marriage and family, he thanked God that God had not answered his high school prayers.

You may have had a flame you thought would be "the one." I did. But after she broke up with me and broke my heart, I fell in love with my best friend, a girl in my youth group named LaVon. We recently celebrated our fortieth anniversary together. Like the song says, I thank God for unanswered prayers.

I've also noted in my life that most of the painful things I've ever experienced, the things I wished God would have miraculously taken away, are the very things that most profoundly shaped my life and made me who I am today. That's true for most people I've spoken with who experienced hardship.

There's a man in the church I serve named Eddie Connor. He lost his wife and two little girls, to cancer. He doesn't believe that God gave his wife and children cancer.

There was a rare genetic condition that neither he nor his wife knew they shared. Two of their four children ended up having the condition, leading to a cancer that is nearly always fatal. Of course, they prayed for healing for their children, and Eddie prayed the same for his wife. But he also understood that God's usual way of working is through people. Eddie also believed God was walking with him and his family through this dark valley.

He described for me a moment when he felt like he could not go on anymore. He was standing at a gas station, and he cried out, "God, I can't do this without you." In that moment he felt the Holy Spirit come over him. He heard God assure him that his wife and daughters would be safe with him, and that Eddie himself was going to be okay. He told me of the sorrow and pain he endured, and the hope his faith gave him, the strength he found from God that carried him.

Eddie also told me how, like Job enduring suffering and loss, he felt God had heard his prayers, had carried him and his surviving children, and ultimately allowed him to meet the woman that would become his second wife, a woman who had, herself, known pain before they met. Together they each found joy once again.

God heard Elizabeth's and Zechariah's prayers all through the years. And God was no doubt moved by their prayers. God walked with them, cared for them, and redeemed their pain, and surprised them in the end, in a way they would never have expected and for purposes they could not have imagined. And God does the same with us.

One last story and we'll move on to the final points in this chapter.

A couple at Church of the Resurrection lost four children to miscarriage. Eventually, they had two successful pregnancies and brought two children into the world. But the couple couldn't shake the feeling that God wanted them to care for foster children as well as their own. They had never met a foster child or foster family before. They took steps and met with a child, but after careful prayer and consideration decided not to bring another child under their roof.

The couple met with a second child and then a third. They began to get the message that this was something God wanted them to do, and they decided to follow God. The couple went through training and, several years ago, they began accepting foster care placements with little children. Since then, they have provided a home for thirty children ranging in age from eight months to three years. In 2017, when they heard that the Kansas Department of Children and Families had teenagers sleeping on the floor of their offices because they lacked placements for all these kids, they decided to do something more.

They called the organization that places kids in Kansas and said they would take in any of these teens at night for whom the department lacked proper accommodations. Soon, this ministry became the focus of their evening work. At last count, in addition to the thirty foster children they have cared for, they have welcomed seven hundred different teens into their home as overnight guests, providing them with a hot meal, a warm bed, a shower, and clean clothes.

This couple eventually bought a home to serve as a group home for teenage girls. This vision started in their hearts when they were enduring miscarriages and feeling the pain of their inability to have children. Out of that loss, they became the answer to the prayers of hundreds of children and teenagers.

The miracles God works sometimes come in ways that are different from what we had imagined when we pray. In this case, there were children praying for a home, and a husband and wife who prayed for a way to make a difference for children. And God answered both of their prayers. As the prophet Malachi had foreseen, God found a way to turn the hearts of adults toward children, and the hearts of children toward adults.

> # God hears our prayers, though God's way of answering them is often different than we sometimes prayed.

All of which is to say that while God isn't closing wombs, or bringing about miscarriages, God has a way of redeeming our pain and forcing good to come from it. God hears our prayers, though God's way of answering them is often different than we sometimes prayed, holding us, walking with us through the pain, and redeeming it in surprising ways.

God Often Chooses and Uses the "Very Old"

There is one last point to be observed from the story of the annunciation and conception of John. It has to do with the age of Elizabeth and Zechariah. I love that as Luke tells this story about them, he tells us that they were "very old." This kind of language would be frowned upon if Luke were writing for the *Washington Post* or *New York Times* today.

The phrase seems a bit insulting. However, it was not meant to be insulting, but to teach something about how God works.

We're not sure how old "very old" was to Luke. In the Bible there is only one time that I can recall that we know the age of someone called "very old." It is in 2 Samuel 19:32, where we read, "Barzillai was very old, 80 years of age." Barzillai had lent his support to King David earlier, but now says that at his age he will be a burden to the king and implies he is nearing death (2 Samuel 19:34-37). In the Jewish Mishna, in a section called "Pirkei Avot" it appears that old age starts at sixty. The Mishnah instructs people to stand to honor someone who is sixty years old or older. As someone quickly approaching sixty, I appreciate the honor given to people at that age, but I'm not ready to accept the moniker of old.

Whatever the age of Elizabeth and Zechariah, the point Luke makes here is a point made throughout scripture, that God often chooses and uses older adults to do God's greatest work. Abraham was seventy-five when God called him to the Promised Land and promised to create a nation through him. Years later, Abraham's wife, Sarah, was ninety when she gave birth to Isaac. Moses was eighty when God called him to lead the Israelite slaves out of captivity. The Bible doesn't know of retirement for anyone except the Levites who carried the Tent of Meeting from place to place. They were to retire at age fifty, but could continue to serve in other ways (Numbers 8:25-26).

In our story today we find God choosing and using an older couple to be a part of his saving plans. Zechariah was surely over fifty, and priests were also Levites, so Zechariah could have been retired, but he chose not to retire. He continued to serve. And while continuing to serve, offering the incense in the Temple, God called him to his greatest adventure yet, to be the father of the prophet who would prepare the way for the Lord.

And even if Zechariah had retired, God's calling doesn't end when we retire; it may be just beginning. Perhaps you are already retired, or you've begun planning or thinking about it. Retirement does not mean an end to God calling you or working in and through you. If your congregation is like mine, you have many people approaching retirement or who are already retired. That represents a *huge opportunity* and an amazing resource of people who have time, wisdom, and life experience waiting to be called and unleashed in ministry.

Several years ago, I met with Pam, at the time recently divorced, and someone who had moved back to Kansas City for a new start. As she began this new chapter in her life, she also felt called to engage in a new mission: to open a home for men and women in recovery or reentering society after time in prison.

Now, Pam runs two homes that provide thirteen people with a warm bed, three meals a day, and a chance at a future with hope. Did I mention that she's in her mid-sixties, likely the age that Zechariah and Elizabeth were when God told them they were receiving both a blessing and a mission? She wasn't trained in this work, but she wasn't too old for it. She felt God calling and said yes.

As Pam and I spoke, she told me her life story. There had been pain and disappointment and heartbreak, just as there had been in the lives of Elizabeth and Zechariah. But she said, "Today, I can look and see how God has used every piece of this to make me who I am today, and to prepare me to do what I'm doing now." There was a joy and light in her eyes as we parted. As she began anew, God gave her a new purpose: to help others begin anew.

Often it is the people who are retired, or older adults, who are most available to God. They have the time, experience, wisdom, passion, and a faith that leads them to say, "Here I am, send me." When I look at the leaders of the church I serve, the choir members, the ushers and greeters, those who serve older adults, those who pack weekend snack packs for hungry children, those who pick up furniture to share in our furnishing ministry for people coming out of homelessness, so many of them are over fifty. And whether you are sixteen or sixty, the point is that we never retire from God's work and that it is in the work that we do to serve God and care for others where we find our greatest joy.

A People Prepared for the Lord

I'd like to end this chapter looking at what Gabriel told Zechariah about the child Elizabeth would bear and his role in God's purposes and plan. In Luke 1:15c-17 we read Gabriel's words about John:

> *"He will be filled with the Holy Spirit even before his birth. He will bring many Israelites back to the Lord their God. He will go forth before the Lord, equipped with the spirit and power of Elijah. He will turn the hearts of fathers back to their children, and he will turn the disobedient to righteous patterns of thinking.* He will make ready a people prepared for the Lord" *(emphasis added).*

We learned in the introduction that when rulers planned to journey to visit cities in their realms, they would send heralds or messengers ahead of them. The aim of these messengers was to ready the people for the monarch's visit. Nearly every ancient culture practiced something like this. Modern heads of state do the same when visiting other cities under their domain.

Malachi, the final book of the Christian Old Testament, repeatedly promised that the Lord would be coming to Jerusalem, to his Temple, and that on that day both judgment and mercy would be meted out. In Malachi 3:1 God says to the people, "Look, I am sending my messenger who will clear the path before me; suddenly the LORD whom you are seeking will come to his temple." While standing in the Temple, Gabriel said, in essence, "Zechariah, your son will be that messenger."

In Malachi 4:1, God says to his people:

Look, the day is coming,
burning like an oven.
All the arrogant ones and all those doing evil will become
straw.
The coming day will burn them,
says the LORD of heavenly forces,
leaving them neither root nor branch.

Judgment is coming to the arrogant, those who do evil, and those who don't revere God, Malachi promises. But for those who repent, those who revere God's name and seek to do God's will, there will be blessings:

The sun of righteousness will rise on those revering my name;
healing will be in its wings
so that you will go forth and jump about like
calves in the stall.

(Malachi 4:2)

27

Judgment and mercy were promised by God through Malachi. A burning oven to destroy, and the warmth of sunshine, healing, and joy to those who revere God's name. But before this day of the Lord's advent, a messenger would come to prepare God's people, to call them to repent and turn to God so that on that day, they might find "healing in its wings" rather than a burning oven.

In case Zechariah still did not understand the role his son was to play, Gabriel makes it even more clear by citing the final words of Malachi,[3]

Look, I am sending Elijah the prophet to you,
before the great and terrifying day of the LORD arrives.
Turn the hearts of the parents to the children
and the hearts of the children to their parents.
(Malachi 4:5-6)

In the light of these closing words of Malachi, listen again to the words of Gabriel to Zechariah in the Temple that day, "[Your son, John] will go forth before the Lord, equipped with the spirit and power of *Elijah*. He will turn the hearts of fathers back to their children, and he will turn the disobedient to righteous patterns of thinking. *He will make ready a people prepared for the Lord*" (Luke 1:17, emphasis added).

To this day, observant Jews end their Sabbath by beckoning Elijah to come, "May Elijah the Prophet come to us, heralding the Messiah, soon and in our days!"[4] And at the Passover Seder, Jewish families have a cup at the table for Elijah, and literally open their door inviting Elijah to enter so that the Messiah might finally arrive.

> **Being ready and being prepared for the Lord involves turning back to one another, turning back to right ways of thinking.**

The angel Gabriel makes clear that John is coming to be the Elijah that Malachi had spoken of more than four hundred years earlier. And for us, today, as in Malachi's day and John's day, being ready and being prepared for the Lord involves turning back to one another, turning back to right ways of thinking. It means turning us toward our children and parents. It means turning us toward God. God says in Malachi 3:7b, "Return to me and I will return to you." This turning, or returning, has a name: repentance.

Earlier in this chapter I shared with you stories of how transformed thinking can turn into transformed actions, one involving a young family who out of their grief and loss came to welcome seven hundred teens in foster care into their home. A second was a retiree who, out of her pain and loss, felt called to open her home to people reentering society after being incarcerated. Not everyone can do this dramatic kind of redemptive work. But we can all do something to foster kindness, to work for justice, to help others see the love of God and draw them back to him.

Several years ago, a high school junior in my congregation stopped me after church.[5] He told me what he was doing at his school as a way of spreading hope and living his faith. He had started a group called Impact of Words. Here's how he explained it in a note he wrote to me:

> Our goal is to spread kindness and love through small messages that we put on people's lockers. Every Wednesday a group of ten people meets after school for 30 minutes, and we write messages to teachers, administrators, students, and faculty. The messages consist of encouragement, gratitude and thankfulness. The idea came to me because of the increased number of suicides in our community.
>
> I was also inspired by going to our church and hearing about trying to make God's kingdom a reality on earth by helping others. We write these messages to spread small acts of kindness

but to also help people that feel depressed, anxious, or isolated to know that they are loved and cared for.

In a sense, Jackson and his friends acted as modern-day John the Baptists—messengers preparing the way for the Lord by helping people remember that their lives matter, that they are loved and valued. They did this by spreading kindness instead of hate or hurt or feelings of worthlessness and despair. They were seeking to help our world look like the kingdom of God; to be filled with people prepared for the Lord. This Advent, what are you doing to prepare the way of the Lord?

Lord, thank you for always hearing my prayers. Thank you for your compassion and love. Please forge from my disappointment and pain something good and beautiful. Help me to be ready to celebrate anew the birth of our Savior, but also to be found ready on that day when you return.

2

PREGNANCY, BIRTH, CIRCUMCISION, AND ZECHARIAH'S PROPHECY

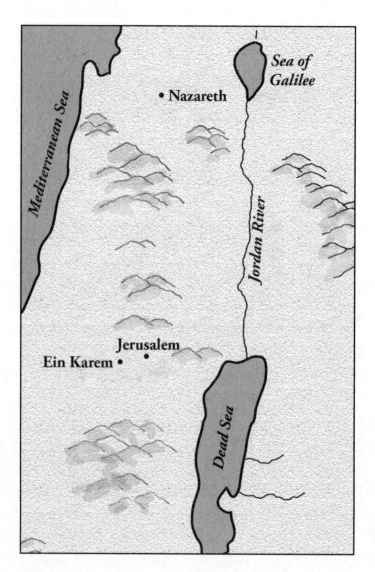

2

PREGNANCY, BIRTH, CIRCUMCISION, AND ZECHARIAH'S PROPHECY

When the time came for Elizabeth to have her child, she gave birth to a boy. Her neighbors and relatives celebrated with her because they had heard that the Lord had shown her great mercy. On the eighth day, it came time to circumcise the child. They wanted to name him Zechariah because that was his father's name. But his mother replied, "No, his name will be John."

They said to her, "None of your relatives have that name." Then they began gesturing to his father to see what he wanted to call him.

After asking for a tablet, he surprised everyone by writing, "His name is John." At that moment, Zechariah was able to speak again, and he began praising God....

Zechariah was filled with the Holy Spirit and prophesied...

"You, child, will be called a prophet of the Most High,
*   for you will go before the Lord to prepare his way.*
You will tell his people how to be saved
*   through the forgiveness of their sins.*
Because of our God's deep compassion,
*   the dawn from heaven will break upon us,*
*   to give light to those who are sitting in darkness*
*   and in the shadow of death,*
*   to guide us on the path of peace."*
*   Luke 1:57-64, 67, 76-79*

How Can I Be Sure?

In the last chapter we left Zechariah in the Holy Place in the Temple conversing with an angel. After hearing Gabriel's amazing announcement that he and Elizabeth would have a child, and that this child would be the long-foretold messenger to come before the Messiah, how did Zechariah respond? With praise and gratitude and celebration? No. Instead he asks Gabriel, "How can I be sure of this?" And Gabriel's response was, in essence, "You cannot be sure; you're going to have to trust."

That is what faith is: trusting in spite of the gnawing questions and doubts that we can't quite banish from our minds.

Sometimes those gnawing questions are meant to prompt us to explore further—and as we do, we sometimes realize that a particular person, belief, or promise is not worthy of our faith. When religion goes wrong, it is often because people have faith in someone or something when they should have paid more attention to their doubts. We are meant to ask questions. Sometimes our doubts are well founded.

When our faith is well placed, our doubts or questions should lead us to a deeper faith.

But when our faith is well placed, our doubts or questions should lead us to a deeper faith. Frederick Buechner once wrote in his book *Wishful Thinking* (HarperOne, 1993), "Doubts are the ants in the pants of faith. They keep it awake and moving."

We all struggle with doubt. Doubt is a normal part of our spiritual life. Martin Luther is said to have noted that "only God and certain madmen have no doubts." Our brains were wired for questioning, for critical thinking, and doubts that inevitably arise are meant to lead us to dig deeper, to search for answers. Zechariah's question, however, points to a truth about life: there are very few things about which we can be absolutely sure. Most decisions we make require a leap of faith.

I remember the night before I married LaVon, I was 83.7 percent sure I was supposed to marry her, that she was the one. I think she was 76.2 percent sure I was the one for her. But despite some uncertainty, we took a leap of faith and we've been married for forty years now.

Our faith in God is much the same. I have reasonable intellectual arguments and meaningful personal experiences that lead me to follow Christ, but in the end it still requires...faith. And it's worth remembering that when Jesus called his first disciples, he didn't say to them, "Set aside all your doubts and uncertainties, don't ask any questions, and come and follow me." Nor did he try to answer all of their questions and explain away all of their doubts. He simply invited them on a journey saying, "Come follow me." That is still his invitation for us today.

The older I am, and the more life I've lived, the deeper my faith and trust in Christ has grown. It is also true that the longer I've lived, the more comfortable I am with uncertainty and the easier I find it to simply trust God without having to be sure. While we, like Zechariah, crave certainty, God gives us mystery and invites us to trust God. So faith is a decision we make, one which we carefully and critically examine, but after having done so, we choose to believe. We choose to follow Christ. This faith, this trusting, is part of what it means to be prepared for the coming of the Lord—it is to choose to trust in him. In Advent we put our trust in the God who came to us in Jesus, as a babe in Bethlehem, and in the hope that one day Christ will return.

Struck Silent

Let's look at Gabriel's response to Zechariah's desire to be sure:

> *Zechariah said to the angel, "How can I be sure of this? My wife and I are very old."*
>
> *The angel replied, "I am Gabriel. I stand in God's presence. I was sent to speak to you and to bring this good news to you. Know this: What I have spoken will come true at the proper time. But because you didn't believe, you will remain silent, unable to speak until the day when these things happen.*
> *(Luke 1:18-20)*

This part of the story makes me smile. The worst thing you can do to a preacher is give her or him some exciting news and a profound experience and then not let the preacher speak! Zechariah has just had the most profound

39

spiritual experience of his life, meeting an angel in the Holy Place of the Temple, and he cannot tell anyone. He has just learned that he and his wife are going to have a baby in their old age. But he can't speak! The old priest will not be able to preach or teach for nine months.

What was this "punishment" about? Was it really a punishment? I don't think so. Rather, I think God was asking Zechariah to talk less and to listen more. I think there is a word for us in here as well. I'm reminded of the words of the psalmist, "Be still, and know that I am God!" (Psalm 46:10 NRSV). I think of the words of Habakkuk the prophet who wrote, "The LORD is in his holy temple. Let all the earth be silent before him" (Habakkuk 2:20). It was in the "sound of sheer silence" (1 Kings 19:12 NRSV) that Elijah the prophet, in his moment of deepest despair, finally heard God.

Each of these passages, interestingly, involved a situation in which people either felt a need to cry out to God or feared that God wasn't listening. Amid the tumult around him, the psalmist looks to God as "a help always near in times of great trouble" (Psalm 46:1). Habakkuk looks upon the evil that seemed pervasive and wants to know why God hasn't brought about fairness and justice. Elijah, who had taken a stand for God, was on the run from the idol-worshipping queen who had vowed to kill him. In each of these instances, God changes the conversation: "Be still,"

God says. "Take a deep breath. Listen. Remember who I am. I have not forgotten you."

The oldest hymn in *The United Methodist Hymnal* dates back to the fourth century, before the date for Christmas was even fixed on the calendar. The hymn, actually a chant that was later set to music, is called "Let All Mortal Flesh Keep Silence." It was a song about the Incarnation, about God's coming to us in Jesus as a babe in Bethlehem. This event is so awe-inspiring, so awe-full, so profound, that the only appropriate response is silence. Take a look at the words:

> Let all mortal flesh keep silence,
> and with fear and trembling stand;
> ponder nothing earthly-minded,
> for with blessing in his hand,
> Christ our God to earth descendeth,
> our full homage to demand.[1]

Several years ago, I took a silent retreat at the Benedictine monastery in Atchison, Kansas. Guests are welcome, the Benedictines are known for their hospitality, but the only time you are allowed to speak during a silent retreat is during mealtimes. For the rest of the day, you remain silent. At first this discipline drove me crazy. I desire sound, I like to be in conversation. I wanted to talk. It took me a full day to get used to the silence. Then I found that, as I was silent,

I began to listen. Sermon ideas began to fill my head. I had dreams and visions for the future of the church I serve, and for my family and in my life. When I turned off the noise and I became silent, I could finally hear the Spirit's whisper. When I listen, I am able to consider points of view I had not considered before. I open my mind to new possibilities.

Perhaps God was silencing Zechariah for a few months so that the priest would be forced to listen, to reorient his thinking, and to pay attention to the amazing thing that God was doing. We see evidence of this in the prophetic words he finally speaks over his newborn son at the end of this period of silence, words we will cover below.

In his epistle, James teaches us this bit of wisdom, one that benefits every relationship we have: "everyone should be quick to listen, slow to speak, and slow to grow angry" (1:19). We've all heard it said that God gave us two ears and one mouth in direct proportion to how much he intends for us to use them. For me, James's words are so important that we had our entire congregation memorize them several years ago. Particularly in our polarized world, silence and listening are important.

Silence is an expression of awe and worship that is an appropriate response to the glory of God. It is in silence that we can hear God speak. Do you take enough time for silence? Do you ever turn off the noise, the radio, the television, your phone and computer and just listen for God to speak? "Let all mortal flesh keep silence…"

Silence is an expression of awe and worship that is an appropriate response to the glory of God. It is in silence that we can hear God speak.

Intimacy and Aging

Once Zechariah had finished his priestly service, he went home, and somehow he explained what happened. What an interesting game of charades that must have been! Then, implicit in Luke's story is that the old priest and his wife, whom Luke calls blameless and righteous, made love. Would you indulge me to chase a rabbit for a moment?

When in church, Christians often speak in hushed tones about sex. Our society seems obsessed with the subject, but in church, we're often silent as if this were a dirty or sinful subject we should not be talking about. Yet within the Bible, intimacy is a gift from God. It is sacred and beautiful. It is at the heart of God's command to humans to "be fruitful and multiply." It is the starting point for every baby born in scripture except Jesus. One entire book of the Bible is dedicated to celebrating intimacy and love (Song of Solomon).

As an interesting sidenote, in Zechariah and Elizabeth's story we have an older couple being intimate. Society often seems uncomfortable with the idea that older adults still share sexual intimacy, and often we don't speak of this. But in this story, as in the story of Abraham and Sarah, an older couple makes love. In Genesis 18:12, when the eighty-nine-year-old Sarah hears that she and her ninety-nine-year-old husband, Abraham, are going to have a baby, she asks, "After I have grown old, and my husband is old, shall I have pleasure?" (NRSV).[2] The pleasure here might have been the pleasure of having a child, but many commentators believe she is referring to the act of making love. The Hebrew word is *ednah*, from the word Eden. Yes, intimacy changes as we age, and making love sometimes means something different in one's eighties than it does in one's twenties, or fifties. But it can still be an important part of life.

Who Is Your Elizabeth? Who Is Your Mary?

Back to the story! Luke 1:24-25 reads, "Afterward, his wife Elizabeth became pregnant. She kept to herself for five months, saying, 'This is the Lord's doing. He has shown his favor to me by removing my disgrace among other people.'" For five months Elizabeth goes into seclusion. Now, both Zechariah and Elizabeth enter a life of quiet. Why? We don't know. Perhaps she worries that she could miscarry as she may have done before and wants to avoid the pain of publicly losing a pregnancy. Perhaps she seeks to savor every moment of the pregnancy. Or maybe she, too, like Zechariah, is seeking silence and quiet, a time to ponder and reflect and listen for God's voice.

In the sixth month of Elizabeth's pregnancy, Mary, Elizabeth's much younger cousin or niece (Luke only tells us they were relatives), is visited by the same angel that had visited Elizabeth. Mary lives seventy miles north of Jerusalem. Gabriel comes to her announcing that she will conceive and bear a son, and she is to name him Jesus. He will be the long-awaited messianic King. Before leaving Mary, Gabriel says to her, "Look, even in her old age, your relative Elizabeth has conceived a son. This woman who was labeled 'unable to conceive' is now six months pregnant. Nothing is impossible for God" (Luke 1:36-37).

It is interesting that, upon learning that she will be pregnant, not having been with a man, Mary's first response is to leave her hometown to visit her cousin or aunt, Elizabeth. "Mary got up and *hurried* to a city in the Judean highlands. She entered Zechariah's home and greeted Elizabeth" (Luke 1:39-40, emphasis added).

Why did Mary leave her hometown so quickly, making a seven-to-eight-day journey on foot, to find Elizabeth? Was she afraid to tell her own parents what the angel had announced to her? Being a pregnant, unmarried teen could result in death. Knowing that Elizabeth was too old to have a child, yet was six months pregnant, did she believe that Elizabeth would understand and believe her story? And, is it possible that Mary had a particularly close relationship with Elizabeth, that she was an older mentor and mother figure for Mary? As we'll see below, that seems likely.

Whatever the reason, let's see what happens when the now pregnant Mary arrives at the home of Elizabeth and Zechariah:

> *She entered the house of Zechariah and greeted Elizabeth. When Elizabeth heard Mary's greeting, the child leaped in her womb. And Elizabeth was filled with the Holy Spirit and exclaimed with a loud cry, "Blessed are you among women, and blessed is the fruit of your womb. And why has this happened to me, that the mother of my Lord comes to me? For as soon as I heard the sound of your greeting, the child in my womb leaped for joy. And blessed is she who believed that there would be a fulfillment of what was spoken to her by the Lord."*

> *(Luke 1:40-45 NRSV)*

Luke notes, throughout this story, the presence and work of the Holy Spirit. Gabriel had promised that Zechariah and Elizabeth's son would be filled with the Holy Spirit even before he was born. Gabriel told Mary she would conceive Jesus when the Holy Spirit came upon her. And now, Elizabeth is filled with the Holy Spirit as she speaks. In the Old Testament the Spirit of God came upon the prophets as they prophesied, upon the great warriors as they fought battles, and upon the king. Here the Holy Spirit comes upon Elizabeth and she, essentially, prophesies. Mary has not yet told her of the pregnancy, but Elizabeth knows. And she does something else. In Luke's Gospel, she becomes the first person to declare that Jesus is Lord: "And why has this happened to me, that the mother of my Lord comes to me?" (Luke 1:43 NRSV).

It was the leaping of the child, of John, in Elizabeth's womb, when Elizabeth and the child first heard Mary's voice, that led Elizabeth to know that Mary was pregnant, and that the child in her womb would be the messianic King. How could Elizabeth know all of that from John leaping in her womb? As we saw in the last chapter, Gabriel had quoted Malachi when telling Zechariah about the identity of the son he and Elizabeth would have:

> *"He will turn many of the people of Israel to the Lord their God. With the spirit and power of Elijah he will go before*

> *him, to turn the hearts of parents to their children, and the*
> *disobedient to the wisdom of the righteous,* to make ready
> a people prepared for the Lord."
> *(Luke 1:16-17 NRSV, emphasis added)*

If Elizabeth's son was to make a people ready for the Lord, then she and Zechariah must have believed, as many did in that day, that the Messiah was coming—and their son would prepare the way.

The Dead Sea Scrolls were written by a sect of Jewish believers known as the Essenes who taught that before the Messiah would come, Elijah would return. The fact that people ask about Elijah through the Gospels tells us many Jewish people had this expectation. And as we learned in the last chapter, Jewish people continue to invite Elijah to join them at the Passover as a way of recognizing this understanding that before the Messiah comes, Elijah will come. Knowing Gabriel had said her son would minister in the spirit and power of Elijah, Elizabeth was waiting and anticipating that the Messiah was coming.

As noted above, Elizabeth is the first person to "confess with [her] mouth that 'Jesus is Lord'" (see Romans 10:9), the fundamental confession of the Christian faith. But her son, John, has already begun preparing the way for Jesus even from within her womb! This is his mission in life and he's begun fulfilling it in the sixth month of Elizabeth's pregnancy.

Elizabeth then shouts with a loud cry words that every Catholic will recognize from the "Hail Mary": "Blessed are you among women, and blessed is the fruit of your womb." (Luke 1:42 NRSV). Elizabeth then blesses Mary again, and the child she carries, noting that when she heard Mary's voice, the child in her womb "leaped for joy."

Elizabeth's story here is an Advent story. She proclaims that Jesus is Lord and that he is a source of our joy. She and John model for us the "good news of great joy for all people" that the angels will proclaim to the shepherds the night that Christ was born.

In response to this remarkable blessing from Elizabeth, and the witness of John's joy from within the womb, Mary moves from fear to rejoicing. For the first time Mary breaks out in song, her Magnificat.

> *My soul magnifies the Lord,*
> *and my spirit rejoices in God my Savior,*
> *for he has looked with favor on the lowliness of his servant.*
> *Surely, from now on all generations will call me blessed;*
> *for the Mighty One has done great things for me,*
> *and holy is his name.*
> *His mercy is for those who fear him*
> *from generation to generation.*
> *He has shown strength with his arm;*
> *he has scattered the proud in the thoughts of their hearts.*
> *He has brought down the powerful from their thrones,*
> *and lifted up the lowly;*

The Church of the Visitation in Ein Karem commemorating Elizabeth and Mary's greeting of Luke 1.

> *he has filled the hungry with good things,*
> *   and sent the rich away empty.*
> *He has helped his servant Israel,*
> *   in remembrance of his mercy,*
> *according to the promise he made to our ancestors,*
> *   to Abraham and to his descendants forever.*
> *   (Luke 1:46-55 NRSV)*

Mary will stay with Elizabeth for the first three months of her pregnancy, which are also the last three months of Elizabeth's pregnancy. Elizabeth is the first to celebrate Mary's pregnancy. Mary is the first person whom Elizabeth

A statue of Elizabeth greeting Mary, outside the Church of the Visitation in Ein Karem.

allows in to break her period of seclusion. These women care for each other, encourage and bless each other, both of them helping and lifting the spirit of the other.

Their relationship represents the loving, caring, mentoring relationship of women for each other: of aunts to their nieces, of friends with friends, of mothers and daughters, grandmothers and granddaughters, of women caring for women. Each helped the other find their joy, each encouraged and cared for the other. And each helped the other to understand God's purposes.

Several years ago, I visited Ein Karem, the traditional site of Elizabeth and Zechariah's home and of John's birth. Most American Protestants don't stop there on their pilgrimages to the Holy Land, but many Catholics make visiting Ein Karem a priority. There they visit the Church of the Visitation, commemorating the visit of Mary to Elizabeth and the story we've just recounted, including Mary's Magnificat. The church is beautiful, completed in 1955 but built atop ruins of previous churches. Outside the church, in its courtyard, is a modern bronze statue of Elizabeth greeting Mary, both women pregnant. It is quite beautiful. On the wall behind it, in dozens of different languages, are ceramic tiles with verses from the Magnificat.

While I was there, four buses arrived, two with African women and the other two with Asian women. I watched as these women came, arm in arm, to the statue of Mary and Elizabeth. Their joy and close relationships seemed to mirror that of Elizabeth and Mary in Luke's Gospel. Some of them asked me if I would take pictures of them standing next to Mary and Elizabeth, and for several minutes I was handed a succession of cameras taking pictures of them before this statue that represented the friendship and love of Mary and Elizabeth. I could see on their faces and in their expressions the joy that Mary spoke of when she was with Elizabeth, "My soul magnifies the Lord, and my spirit rejoices in God my Savior" (Luke 1:46b-47 NRSV).

I thought of so many women in the congregation I serve who have been an Elizabeth for a younger woman, or younger women who have been a Mary to someone older. We all need relationships like this in our lives. As I write these words, one of the saints of my church has recently died. Betty spoke with a southern drawl and always called me "Honey." Her words have always been so life-giving to me and to so many others. And though she'd battled dementia for several years, she still called everyone "Honey" and expressed a beautiful love to them, even when she could not remember their names. She was an example of a modern-day Elizabeth.

Bear in mind that Mary didn't decide to travel eight days to Ein Karem to spend time with a distant relative she didn't know well. This visit points to a deep relationship that likely formed when Mary was a little girl, on visits to Jerusalem. I wonder if you have an aunt or uncle or grandparent that you had a special relationship with. Or maybe it was a Sunday school teacher or youth group leader who invested in your life as you were growing up—someone you came to trust, who you knew you could go to if you needed help. Everyone needs an Elizabeth, but as we grow older, we also find ourselves needing a Mary.

> ## Everyone needs an Elizabeth, but as we grow older, we also find ourselves needing a Mary.

Such relationships, which help form dense networks of caring, are of course not limited to women. Men need them as well. We might be an older Paul or a young Timothy, a mature Barnabas or a young John Mark, but whatever our age, we all benefit from these kinds of relationships. They are part of what it means to live our faith in community rather than as isolated individuals.

When I first started the Church of the Resurrection, I was twenty-five years old, and I benefited from men who were like fathers to me. They'd take me to lunch, offer encouragement when I was discouraged. When I needed help, I knew I could call them. By the time I was in my thirties I was being asked to speak at conferences but was struggling with the time commitment. Particularly challenging were those within driving distance, less than four hours away. I would drive to the conference, speak over the course of an afternoon and evening, and again the next morning, then drive home. But I still needed to prepare a sermon for the weekend, along with whatever other meetings I'd have when I got back to the office. Independently of one another, two men, Chuck Bloom and Jack Highfill, both reached out to say that they wanted to drive me on these trips so I could work in the car.

I changed my pace in doing conferences after a few years, but I will never forget what these guys did, and how in this, and so many other ways, they encouraged and cared for me. They are now in their eighties, but they still find ways to encourage and bless me. But what struck me as I was writing this chapter is that I've not been nearly as good a Mary or a Timothy to them as they've been serving as an

Elizabeth or a Paul to me. I wonder if you have an older adult who played, and perhaps continues to play, the role of Elizabeth in your life, who may need you to be a better Mary. Or if there are younger Timothys in your sphere of influence who need you to be a Paul. Are you investing in relationships with older and younger people? Who is your Elizabeth? Who is your Mary?

His Name Is John

Luke goes on to describe the birth of John, just as he narrates the birth of Jesus six months later:

> *When the time came for Elizabeth to have her child, she gave birth to a boy. Her neighbors and relatives celebrated with her because they had heard that the Lord had shown her great mercy. On the eighth day, it came time to circumcise the child. They wanted to name him Zechariah because that was his father's name. But his mother replied, "No, his name will be John."*
>
> *They said to her, "None of your relatives have that name." Then they began gesturing to his father to see what he wanted to call him.*
>
> *After asking for a tablet, he surprised everyone by writing, "His name is John." At that moment, Zechariah was able to speak again, and he began praising God.*
>
> *(Luke 1:57-64)*

The angel told Zechariah the name God had chosen for this child, who would be a messenger going before the Messiah. The name John, in Hebrew, is *Johanan*, which means, "The Lord is gracious." The angel also revealed to Mary the name she was to give to her child: Jesus, in Hebrew, *Yeshua*, which means "The Lord saves." Their names are important to their mission, and both tell us about God. But I want to focus on John here.

God is gracious—the Greek word behind grace and gracious, *charis*, appears more than 150 times in the New Testament. It translates into English as kindness, favor, undeserved blessings that are extended to another simply due to the goodness of the giver, not because the recipient deserves it. It is what you embody when you help a complete stranger. It is particularly evident when you are kind to someone who has wronged you. Christians believe that grace, along with its partners, love and justice, are the defining characteristics of God.

God is gracious. God seeks to show kindness and mercy to the human race, which is precisely why God came to us in the person of Jesus. And Johanan, "God is Gracious," was sent by God because of God's grace, to prepare the way for the Lord's advent by inviting people to repent, returning to God and to one another. We'll focus on John's message in the remaining chapters in the book. But here I simply want us to see in his name a preview of what it means to prepare the way of the Lord. It is both to receive and to give grace. This is the rhythm of the Christian life. We accept God's love, and we reflect God's love. We receive God's kindness, and we in turn live that kindness toward others. Receiving then giving, accepting then reflecting.

God is gracious. God seeks to show kindness and mercy to the human race.

I'm reminded of the words of Paul, who wrote,

For by grace you have been saved through faith, and this is not your own doing; it is the gift of God—not the result of works, so that no one may boast. For we are what he has made us, created in Christ Jesus for good works, which God prepared beforehand to be our way of life.
(Ephesians 2:8-10 NRSV)

We are saved *by* God's grace—by God's undeserved kindness. But we are also saved *for* a purpose: to share and live that kindness toward others, to pass on God's love and grace to others. We are saved *by* grace, and we are saved *for* good works, which are themselves a form of grace.

Several years ago, I watched the funeral of former President George H. W. Bush. I was particularly touched by the eulogy that his son, former President George W. Bush, delivered for his father. At one point he described his father in terms that reminded me of the mentoring role of Elizabeth to Mary, saying that his father,

> Nurtured and honored many—his many friendships with a generous and giving soul. There exists thousands of handwritten notes encouraging or sympathizing or thanking his friends and acquaintances. He had an enormous capacity to give of himself. Many a person would tell you that Dad became a mentor and a father figure in their life.

The younger Bush then choked up as he spoke his final words about his father, words that I found most moving. He described the elder Bush in ways that reflected God's graciousness lived out in a human life. Quoting his father's inaugural address he said,

> We cannot hope only to leave our children a bigger car, a bigger bank account. We must hope to give them a sense of what it means to be a loyal friend, a loving parent, a citizen who leaves his home, his neighborhood, and town better than he found it. What do we want the men and women who work with us to say when we are no longer there? That we were

more driven to succeed than anyone around us? Or that we stopped to ask if a sick child had gotten better, and stayed a moment there to trade a word of friendship?

Well, Dad, we're going to remember you for exactly that and much more.

And we are going to miss you. Your decency, sincerity, and kind soul will stay with us forever.[3]

Whether you are a Democrat, Republican, or Independent, you can see in this son's words about his father, a picture of grace, of seeking to live your life more concerned with serving others than with being served.

A Father's Prophetic Word

Just after Zechariah affirmed that his son's name would be John, he was able to speak, after nine months of silence! He begins praising God, then Luke writes:

All their neighbors were filled with awe, and everyone throughout the Judean highlands talked about what had happened. All who heard about this considered it carefully. They said, "What then will this child be?" Indeed, the Lord's power was with him.

(Luke 1:65-66)

What then will this child be? That is the question Zechariah answers when the Holy Spirit comes upon him and he begins to prophesy, offering a beautiful song, in some ways parallel to Mary's Magnificat:

"Bless the Lord God of Israel
> *because he has come to help and has delivered his people.*
He has raised up a mighty savior for us in his servant David's house,
> *just as he said through the mouths of his holy prophets long ago.*
He has brought salvation from our enemies
> *and from the power of all those who hate us.*
He has shown the mercy promised to our ancestors,
> *and remembered his holy covenant,*
>> *the solemn pledge he made to our ancestor Abraham.*
He has granted that we would be rescued
> *from the power of our enemies*
so that we could serve him without fear,
> *in holiness and righteousness in God's eyes,*
>> *for as long as we live.*
You, child, will be called a prophet of the Most High,
> *for you will* go before the Lord to prepare his way.
You will tell his people how to be saved
> *through the forgiveness of their sins.*
Because of our God's deep compassion,
> the dawn from heaven will break upon us,
> *to give light to those who are sitting in darkness*
> *and in the shadow of death,*
>> *to guide us on the path of peace."*

(Luke 1:68-79, emphasis added)

Luke cites these beautiful words to ensure that his readers know who John the Baptist is and why he has come. This prophetic word captures the Advent message of John the Baptist. It summarizes what Advent is all about and gives a preview of things to come in Luke's Gospel. This song contains allusions to eighteen different Old Testament texts from the Law, the Prophets, and the Writings—all three major sections of the Tanakh, the Old Testament.

Notice it begins by affirming that God has come to help and deliver his people. We might expect him to say that God is coming, not that he has come. But remember, Mary has lived with them three months and shared with them what Gabriel had told her about her son (who is to be named *Yeshua*, "Yahweh saves"). John had leapt in Elizabeth's womb upon hearing Mary's voice. Elizabeth, filled with the Holy Spirit, had already foreseen the child in Mary's womb would be the Lord. The Greek word for help and deliver that Zechariah uses as he begins his prophetic word is *lutrosin*, which actually means "redeemed" or "redemption" or also "ransomed." The word was often used of purchasing the freedom of a slave, or ransoming someone held in captivity. These ideas show up in the prophets, but they are also central to how Christians understood Jesus's death: as a ransom or act of redemption.

Zechariah goes on to prophesy that God has "raised up a mighty savior" from David's house. He's clear that this savior, through whom God comes to redeem his people, will be a descendant of David, as Jesus would be. Zechariah seems to have the same expectations most Jews who were awaiting the coming of the Messiah had in that time, namely, that the Messiah would rescue and redeem and save the Jewish people from the Romans and "all those who hate us." All of this was because God remembered the covenant with God's people.

But after speaking to the salvation that was coming through Mary's child, Zechariah turns to the role his son Johanon will play in God's redemptive plans. "You, child, will be called a prophet of the Most High, for you will *go before the Lord to prepare his way*" (Luke 1:76, emphasis added). Here he cites Malachi 3:1: "I am sending my messenger to prepare the way before me" (NRSV). He will prepare them by calling them to repent, to return to God and in so doing, to receive his forgiveness.

I love what Luke writes in verse 78, "Because of our God's deep compassion, *the dawn from heaven will break upon us*" (emphasis added). God's deep compassion. *Deep* in Greek refers to one's most inward parts—one's heart, the seat of one's affections. It is God's visceral compassion, his heartfelt compassion, his tender mercy that is at play in this unfolding plan. I so love this picture of God's deeply rooted, keenly felt compassion for us. Notice it is because of God's deep compassion that, "the dawn from heaven will break upon us." Malachi says it this way referring to the coming of the Lord: "the sun of righteousness will rise on those revering my name; healing will be in its wings" (4:2).

This is Advent, when the dawn from heaven breaks upon us, regardless of the darkness we've been living in. It is the sun of righteousness rising with healing in its wings.

We observe Advent during the month with the longest nights of the year. Darkness continues to conquer the daylight during December. Early Christians did not know when Jesus was born and when the date for Christmas was fixed in the West, it was set for the day when sunlight began to push back the darkness, the day after the longest night of the year. In the Julian calendar that was December 25 (in 1582 Pope Gregory XIII reformed the calendar which leads to the longest night, the winter solstice, now occurring around December 21).

At Christmas Eve candlelight services in many churches, we tell the Christmas story, then at the climax of the service, we extinguish all the lights in the room, and extinguish the Advent candles. We sit in the darkness for a moment. We feel the discomfort of the darkness. We yearn for the light. We then bring in the Christ candle, representing Jesus whose birth we've come to celebrate. At Church of the Resurrection, we often invite families to do this who have experienced adversity, grief, or some other kind of loss through the year, but who have survived.

Last year, a woman named Darlene walked down the aisle with her children and grandchildren. Her husband, Max, had contracted COVID-19 and died earlier in the year. She approached the altar and lit the large Christ candle. From the Christ candle I lit my candle, then shared the light with each of her family members, then lit the candles of our pastors, who began lighting the candles of others until the sanctuary was filled with light. There were tears in Darlene's eyes, but as she watched the room fill with light, she knew the truth: in Christmas the dawn from heaven breaks upon us, the sun of righteousness has come with healing in its wings.

John came to prepare the way. And Christ, in his Advent, came...

> *Because of our God's deep compassion,*
>> *the dawn from heaven will break upon us,*
>> *to give light to those who are sitting in darkness*
>> *and in the shadow of death,*
>>> *to guide us on the path of peace.*
>>> *(Luke 1:78-79, emphasis added)*

Lord, help me to trust you, even when I am not sure. Help me to find moments of silence to listen for your voice and reflect on my need for your grace and light. Use me as an Elizabeth for some, and a Mary for others, encouraging and being encouraged. And thank you for bringing the dawn from on high to break upon me. Help me to walk in the light of your love.

3

JOHN'S MINISTRY AND PREACHING

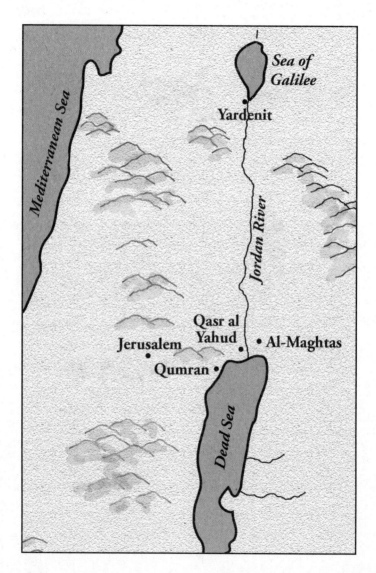

3

JOHN'S MINISTRY AND PREACHING

[John] grew up, becoming strong in character. He was in the wilderness until he began his public ministry to Israel . . .

In the fifteenth year of the rule of the emperor Tiberius . . . God's word came to John son of Zechariah in the wilderness. John went throughout the region of the Jordan River, calling for people to be baptized to show that they were changing their hearts and lives and wanted God to forgive their sins. This is just as it was written in the scroll of the words of Isaiah the prophet,

A voice crying out in the wilderness:
"Prepare the way for the Lord."

Luke 1:80; 3:1a, 2b-4

John wore clothes made of camel's hair, with a leather belt around his waist. He ate locusts and wild honey.

People from Jerusalem, throughout Judea, and all around the Jordan River came to him. As they confessed their sins, he baptized them in the Jordan River.

Matthew 3:4-6

Then John said to the crowds who came to be baptized by him, "You children of snakes! Who warned you to escape from the angry judgment that is coming soon? Produce fruit that shows you have changed your hearts and lives."

Luke 3:7-8

Luke devotes sixty-three verses to telling the story of John's conception and birth, twenty-two verses to John's preaching and baptizing ministry, including the baptism of Jesus, and twenty-nine additional verses that mention John. For that reason we've spent the first half of this book focused on the stories surrounding John's birth. In this chapter we'll turn to John's preaching and baptizing ministry, and in the last chapter, we'll focus on the other things the Gospels tell us about John's life, death, and legacy.

In this chapter we'll briefly cover what we can surmise from scripture about the years between John's birth and the beginning of his public ministry in "the fifteenth year of the rule of emperor Tiberius." Then we'll turn to John's message and ministry and how it not only prepared his hearers for the coming of Jesus, but how it still prepares us to celebrate Christ's first advent, and is pivotal in making us ready for Christ's second advent.

John the Baptist and the Dead Sea Scrolls

After describing the events leading up to John's birth, Luke summarizes his childhood and young adulthood with these words: "The child grew up, becoming strong in character. He was in the wilderness until he began his public ministry to Israel" (Luke 1:80). That's all we have in the Gospels of John's life from his circumcision on the eighth day after he was born until he begins his public ministry at the age of thirty.

Luke doesn't mention John's parents after his circumcision, and they are nowhere mentioned in the other Gospels. Recall that Luke tells us they were very old. Perhaps they died when John was young. It is also possible that his parents dedicated him to God, and, at an early age, took him to live in a religious community to be trained for God's work. This is exactly what happened with Samuel, a prophet and the last of the judges who lived 1,100 years before John was born. Like John, Samuel's parents had been unable to conceive, but then they miraculously conceived a child and dedicated him to God. And when Samuel was just a boy they took him to the local priest at Shiloh, a man named Eli, and they entrusted Samuel to Eli who would raise and mentor Samuel to prepare him to give spiritual leadership to Israel (you can read that story in 1 Samuel 1:21-28).

In the same way, some believe that John was taken by his parents to a community of Jewish priests and scribes living just east of Jerusalem, on the northwest shore of the Dead Sea. This community had devoted themselves to preparing for the coming of the Messiah.

The community is known as Qumran, and the Jewish group most believe lived there were called Essenes.[1] They were known to have taken in boys and young men who were orphaned, or dedicated to God by their parents, training them in the faith. They understood themselves to be doing what Isaiah 40:3 foretold, "A voice cries out: 'In the wilderness prepare the way of the LORD'" (NRSV).

Luke notes that John "grew up, becoming strong in character. He was in the wilderness until he began his public ministry to Israel." Based on this it seems likely to many that John grew up among the Essenes, rather than in the "hill country of Judea" where he had been born. The fact that John, when asked by the religious leaders about his identity, replied, "I am the voice of one crying out in the wilderness," just as the Essene community understood themselves to be,

A Dead Sea Scroll fragment.

is one more among many connections between John and the Essenes.

The Essenes practiced ritual bathing—baptism—for purification. They carefully studied scripture and sought to live holy, devout lives. They lived simply, and they sought to withdraw from the sinfulness of the world. They believed the Messiah was soon to come (or possibly messiahs; it appears the Essenes may have expected more than one messianic figure). They believed in a coming apocalyptic battle between the sons of light and the sons of darkness.

This community is believed to have produced the hundreds of documents we know as the Dead Sea Scrolls, hiding them in the caves in the limestone cliffs surrounding Qumran as the Roman armies were marching their direction in AD 68. The Essenes fled before the Romans arrived. Their community was destroyed, but the scrolls remained hidden in the caves until the first scroll was discovered by a Bedouin boy in late 1946, one of the most important archaeological discoveries in history.

I've been to Qumran many times, and each time I'm there, as I walk among the remains of the buildings

Qumran Cave 4, where the majority of the Dead Sea Scrolls were discovered.

on the archaeological site, I can't help but wonder if I'm walking where John walked and seeing what he saw. Is his handwriting preserved on any of the Dead Sea Scrolls that have been discovered? It's a tantalizing possibility.

We know from the writings of the first-century Jewish historian Josephus that the Essenes took in children and young men who were either orphaned or dedicated to God by their parents. But that doesn't prove that John lived with the Essenes. Yet as we read more about what the Essenes believed and practiced, and as scholars have studied those Dead Sea Scrolls that describe the beliefs and practices of the people who composed them, we see many similarities

A Mikva at Qumran where the Essenes practiced ritual bathing.

between this Jewish sect and John's life and ministry as recounted in the Gospels.

Both John and the Essenes lived an ascetic lifestyle. Both the Essenes and John believed the Messiah was coming soon. Both saw themselves fulfilling the words of Isaiah, who had foretold "A voice cries out: 'In the wilderness prepare the way of the LORD'" (Isaiah 40:3 NRSV). Both John and the Essenes practiced baptism for purification and forgiveness from sin. Both the Essenes and John called for sharing one's personal possessions with others in the community. Both ate simply, dressed simply (though John wore camel skin, the Essenes a simple white robe), and eschewed marriage

73

for themselves (though some Essenes did marry, it was not the norm). Both believed and sought to live a life of radical devotion to God. There is a remarkable similarity between what we know of John the Baptist and what we know of the Essenes at Qumran.

There are also some key differences between John and the Essenes. Most notably, the Essenes were an exclusive community that sought to separate themselves from all they considered sinful. They required adherence to a strict set of rules and a multiyear process before one could become a part of their community.

Compare that with John the Baptist, who, Luke says, "went throughout the region of the Jordan River, calling for people to be baptized to show that they were changing their hearts and lives and wanted God to forgive their sins" (3:3). In Luke 3 we find crowds of people who felt alienated from God, including tax collectors and even soldiers, coming to be baptized by John. This would seem to have been unthinkable to the Essenes.

It seems likely, if John had been a part of the community of the Essenes, that he came to a fundamental difference of opinion with them regarding God's mission—separation and exclusion or reaching out to sinners and inclusion—that led to a parting of the ways. John no longer followed their program of holiness. In a sense, he had "gone rogue."

John seemed to be driven by the idea that God cared for sinners, wanted to forgive them and rescue them, and his mission was to draw people to God, calling them to repent (to change their mind, their hearts, and their actions) as a way of preparing for the Lord. The Essenes, by contrast, seemed to focus on God's judgment of sinners. As the Essenes saw it, God wanted to separate himself from sinners. It followed, then, that if they wanted to live by God's intentions, they should separate themselves from sinners too.

> The question for Christians in the twenty-first century is whether the church is a hospital for sinners or an exclusive club for saints.

Why should we care about this theological difference between a first-century community of ascetic Jews and John the Baptist? Because that difference still plays itself out in religion today. The question for Christians in the twenty-first century is whether the church is a hospital for sinners or an exclusive club for saints. In spite of what John taught and Jesus practiced, many Christian communities today still seem to side with the Essenes in this debate.

I have, from time to time, had people tell me about the sinfulness of this or that person they'd seen at Church of the Resurrection. Did you know that so-and-so is a drunk? Pastor, are you aware that this person had an affair? I heard him or her swear like a sailor. Do you know what kind of people you have attending Resurrection?

My response to these comments varies. Sometimes I'll say something like, "Can you think of anyone who more needs the good news of forgiveness and reconciliation?" Other times I will say "I'm so glad we are a church that draws people like this to Christ!" or simply, "Have you read about the people Jesus called friends?"

Contrast these church attenders with the mindset of Jesus, who, seeing a Samaritan woman who had been divorced five times and was, at the time, living with a man outside of wedlock, offered her living water and called her to be his first missionary to the Samaritans. Or Jesus's embrace of Zacchaeus, a tax collector and sinner, with whom he broke bread and pronounced God's affirmation. Or the "sinful woman" in Luke 7 who wept at Jesus's feet while he ate at the home of Simon the Pharisee. Jesus extended forgiveness and grace to her and to so many in the Gospels.

Malachi foretold a day of judgment. But before that day, God would send his messenger before him to prepare the way. He said, "Return to me and I will return to you" (Malachi 3:1, 7b). In Malachi, God said he would send Elijah before him, to "turn the hearts of the parents to the children and the hearts of the children to their parents" (Malachi 4:5-6). John thought that this was his calling, to prepare the way of the Lord by beckoning the people back to God.

Listen to how Matthew introduces John's ministry, citing the prophet Isaiah:

In those days John the Baptist appeared in the desert of Judea announcing, "Change your hearts and lives! Here comes the kingdom of heaven!" He was the one of whom Isaiah the prophet spoke when he said:

The voice of one shouting in the wilderness,
> *"Prepare the way for the Lord;*
> *make his paths straight."*

(Matthew 3:1-3)

We see John's passion. He's going before the Lord, calling people to be ready. Come on! Hurry! The reign of God (the kingdom of heaven) is coming! His preaching and his baptism were all about preparing the way for the Lord.

Notice what Matthew says next. "John wore clothes made of camel's hair, with a leather belt around his waist" (Matthew 3:4). Why did Matthew feel the need to tell us about John's clothing? Let's look at 2 Kings 1:8 where we hear about the clothing Elijah the prophet wore: "clothes made of hair with a leather belt around his waist." Matthew wants to make sure we see the sign that John was giving to his hearers. John wore the clothes Elijah wore. Why? To make sure they understood that he was the one of whom God said in Malachi 4:5, "Look, I am sending Elijah the prophet to you, before the great and terrifying day of the LORD arrives."

How glad I am that John left the Essenes and their religious exclusivism; that he read Malachi to mean that God did not want to destroy sinners, but to call them to repentance. And how grateful I am that Jesus, like John, came, "Not to call the righteous but sinners." Johanan— Yahweh is Gracious—understood the meaning of his name and chose to embody it in his life and ministry.

Repent: A Change of Mind, Heart, and Actions

Luke tells us that John began his public ministry "in the fifteenth year of the rule of the emperor Tiberius" (3:1).

Tiberius began to reign in AD 14, so the fifteenth year would be AD 29. John was likely born a year or two before Herod's death in 4 BC, perhaps in 6 or 5 BC, making John thirty-five or thirty-six years old when he began his ministry.[2] Dressed as the prophet Elijah, John baptized people in the Jordan. Those who were expecting Malachi's Elijah spread the word. Matthew notes, "People from Jerusalem, throughout Judea, and all around the Jordan River came to him. As they confessed their sins, he baptized them in the Jordan River" (Matthew 3:5-6).

Let's consider what John was preaching out in the wilderness. Again, Matthew summarizes John's message with these words: "In those days John the Baptist appeared in the desert of Judea announcing, 'Change your hearts and lives! Here comes the kingdom of heaven!'" (3:1-3).

The Greek word translated in the Common English Bible as "change your hearts and lives!" is *metanoia*. It is usually translated as "repent." But in the Greek the word is much richer and more complex. It literally means "to think differently afterwards" or to "change your mind." It suggests seeing things so differently that it leads to a change of heart and ultimately a change of behavior. Which of us doesn't need to repent regularly?

You may know that the Greek word for sin in the New Testament is *hamartia*, which means to "miss the mark." It was an archery term that applied to an arrow that fell short of, or veered to the right or left of its intended target. It implies that there is a path we're meant to follow, a target or standard we are meant to uphold, or an ideal way we are meant to live by. To sin is to waver from that path or fall short of that standard.

It doesn't matter whether you are an atheist or agnostic, a Hindu or a Buddhist, a Muslim or Jew or Christian, we all recognize that we miss the mark at times in our lives. We think, say, and do things we should not think, say, or do. We fail to say, think, or do the things we should think, say, or do. We've all blown it when it comes to our relationships with others and our relationship with God. I have, you have, we all have.

I find it helpful, when reflecting on my own sins, to ponder the "seven deadly sins." These were seen as the cardinal or foundational sins from which all others spring. Interestingly, the idea of the seven deadly sins took shape from the work of the Christian monks, who like the Jewish monastics of Qumran, went to live in the desert for solitude and contemplation. These became known as the Desert Fathers, and in some cases, the Desert Mothers. As I list the seven deadly sins, I'd invite you to join me in contemplating, perhaps putting a check mark by, those you may struggle with in one form or another:

- Gluttony
- Lust
- Greed
- Indifference
- Anger
- Envy
- Pride

I've wrestled with them all at one point or another in my life.

Once more we hear John preaching in the wilderness: "Change your hearts and lives! Here comes the kingdom of heaven!" When it comes to repentance and expressing true and heartfelt regret to God, I find it helps sometimes to write a letter, a confession, to God. I wonder if you might want to take a break from reading the rest of this chapter in order to write a prayer of confession to God.

John's aim was to help his hearers be ready for the day of the Lord. We use Advent as an opportunity for spiritual preparation as we anticipate celebrating Christ's first coming, and ready ourselves for his final return for us. Remember God's invitation in Malachi as he spoke of sending a messenger before him: "Return to me and I will return to you" (Malachi 3:7b).

If twenty-first-century Americans were standing near the Jordan River listening to John preach, what do you think he would say to us? What would he ask our polarized society? What message would he bring to our materialistic world? In our shallow, superficial, and self-absorbed society, how would John challenge us? In our sexually obsessed culture, of what might he call us to repent?

"Produce Fruit Worthy of Repentance!"

Throughout most of this book so far, we've looked at John's story mostly through the eyes of Luke's Gospel. Now, we'll turn to Matthew's account to focus on the response to John's message:

> *People from Jerusalem, throughout Judea, and all around the Jordan River came to him. As they confessed their sins, he baptized them in the Jordan River. Many Pharisees and Sadducees [religious leaders] came to be baptized by John. He said to them, "You children of snakes! Who warned you to escape from the angry judgment that is coming soon? Produce fruit that shows you have changed your hearts and lives."*
>
> *(Matthew 3:5-8)*

There's a subtle difference between Matthew's telling of this story and Luke's. Here's how Luke relates the same event in Luke 3:7-8: "Then John said to the crowds who came to be baptized by him, 'You children of snakes! Who warned you to escape from the angry judgment that is coming soon? Produce fruit that shows you have changed your hearts and lives.'"

Did you notice the difference? Matthew notes that John saw the religious leaders coming to him, along with the ordinary sinners. But it is the Pharisees and Sadducees that John called "children of snakes." These were the most overtly religious people, yet John calls them snakes!

Are there any unique temptations that religiously committed people might struggle with that nonreligious people might not? In Jesus's ministry, he never chastises ordinary sinners, but regularly castigates the religious leaders, speaking of them as "blind guides leading the blind." In Matthew 23, Jesus speaks what are sometimes called "the seven woes." Seven times he says, "Woe to you, scribes and Pharisees, hypocrites!" In verses 27-28 he says, "Woe to you, scribes and Pharisees, hypocrites! For you are like whitewashed tombs, which on the outside look beautiful, but inside they are full of the bones of the dead and of all kinds of uncleanness. So you also on the outside look righteous to others, but inside you are full of hypocrisy and lawlessness" (NRSV).

Today, the word *Pharisee* has come to be synonymous with religious hypocrisy (there were many Pharisees that were undoubtedly pious and devout, but so many seemed to be corrupt that Jesus routinely spoke harsh words about them). You may recall the etymology of the word, *hypocrite*. It is a transliteration of the Greek word, *hypokrites*, which meant an actor. Actors often wore masks on stage in order to pretend to be someone they were not. Are you ever tempted to pretend to be someone you are not? Do you ever struggle with hypocrisy?

"Change your hearts and lives! Here comes the kingdom of heaven!"

Returning to Luke's account of John's message, John doesn't single out the religious leaders, but says to everyone in the crowd who came to hear him:

> *"You children of snakes! Who warned you to escape from the angry judgment that is coming soon? Produce fruit that shows you have changed your hearts and lives. And don't even think about saying to yourselves, Abraham is our father. I tell you that God is able to raise up Abraham's children from these stones. The ax is already at the root of the trees. Therefore, every tree that doesn't produce good fruit will be chopped down and tossed into the fire."*
>
> *(Luke 3:7b-9)*

John did not sugarcoat his preaching. And his passion, conviction, and harsh words were intended to shake the crowd up. With the Holy Spirit working through him, it had the desired effect. This led the crowd to ask, "What then should we do?" In essence, what does the good fruit of repentance that God desires actually look like? John responded,

> *"Whoever has two shirts must share with the one who has none, and whoever has food must do the same."*

> *Even tax collectors came to be baptized. They said to him, "Teacher, what should we do?"*

> *He replied, "Collect no more than you are authorized to collect."*

> *Soldiers asked, "What about us? What should we do?"*

> *He answered, "Don't cheat or harass anyone, and be satisfied with your pay."*

> *(Luke 3:11-14)*

What does the good fruit of repentance that God desires actually look like?

I find John's answers interesting for a couple of reasons. First, notice that John defines the fruit of repentance only in terms of action. You may recall here that the Greek word we translate as "repent" involves changed hearts and minds leading to changed actions. John goes straight to the bottom line: our repentance will be assessed by what we do, the fruit we bear, and not just what we claim to believe or feel in our hearts. In his Sermon on the Mount, Jesus echoes John when he says that not everyone who calls out "Lord, Lord" will enter the kingdom of heaven, but only those who *do* (emphasis added) the will of the Father.

The other thing I find so interesting about John's statements is that all the fruit of repentance, the evidence that our hearts are spiritually preparing for the Kingdom and the coming King, have to do with economics and compassion. Did you notice that? To the crowds he said to share clothes and food with those who don't have enough. To the tax collectors, John says: "Don't rip people off, don't gouge people, don't overcharge people." (A common complaint in John's day was that tax collectors, acting within Rome's authority, abused their power, collecting more in taxes they should have, thereby enriching themselves.) To the Roman soldiers who have come to be baptized, John says: "Don't cheat and harass people but be content with what you have." Stop here just for a moment and think about this remarkable image of despised Roman occupiers and their collaborators, the hated tax collectors, responding to the call to repentance and receiving baptism, right alongside the Jewish inhabitants of Judea living under that occupation.

Knowing John's message was focused on addressing greed and the abuse of power and called his hearers to generosity and justice, what would John say if he were preaching in America today?

Like most congregations, one focus of Advent at the Church of the Resurrection is calling people to serve others and to generosity. It seeks to act as a counterbalance when so much of the buildup to Christmas is focused on conspicuous consumerism. We invite people to demonstrate fruits of repentance, of a transformed mind and heart and pocketbook, through selfless acts of service, compassion, and generosity toward those in need. Our goal is that this becomes the rhythm of our lives throughout the year, but Advent is a great place to start.

Most in our congregation already have more than they need, and if they have children or grandchildren, their kids have more than they need. Focusing on giving and sharing and serving, and inviting our congregants to do the same with their families, actually serves as an antidote to the materialism often experienced in the season, and in the process, brings greater joy. I've always loved pastor Mike Slaughter's admonition that, "Christmas is not *your* birthday."

Last Advent we invited our congregation to help with two dozen different projects benefiting low-income children and their families, half in Kansas City, half in the developing world. One of the projects was giving funds to purchase goats for families in Haiti. The hope was to purchase a male and female goat for each family, and these goats would breed and produce more goats. The goats provided milk, and, eventually, food, for the recipients of these gifts. Each goat cost $100, and we invited people to purchase a part of a goat, and entire goat, or multiple goats.

After worship one Sunday, a nine-year-old girl named Rose came to me and said, "Pastor Adam, I'd like to buy a goat for a family in Haiti." She was excited and so earnest. I knelt by her and said, "That's terrific Rose! That will really make a difference for a family in Haiti." She handed me two fifty dollar bills and together we got an offering envelope, wrote her name on the envelope, designating the enclosed funds to buy a goat. I said, "Rose, I'm so proud of you." But then I made a terrible mistake. Assuming that a nine-year-old would not have one hundred dollars to give, I asked, "Did your Mom and Dad help with this too?" To which Rose replied, "No, Pastor Adam, this is the money I got for my birthday. I wanted to use it to help other children." I wanted to cry as she told me this. Here was a nine-year-old girl who understood what Advent and Christmas was all about—what it meant to prepare the way of the Lord.

Thinking about the kind of fruit John called his hearers to bear takes us back to one of the most beloved passages of the Hebrew Bible, Micah 6:8. I suspect that many of you know this text by heart. Here's what Micah says about living according to God's will: "He has told you, human one, what is good and what the LORD requires from you: to do justice, embrace faithful love, and walk humbly with your God." Faithful love, in Hebrew, is *hesed*, which is often translated as kindness or goodness. As Micah explained, it wasn't rule-following that God was looking for; it was mercy, compassion, and humility. All of these attributes involve how we relate to others and to God. It was the lack of these things, in part, that led John to call people to repentance.

John's message, and Micah's too, closely mirror what Jesus called the two greatest commandments: love God with your entire being, and love your neighbor as you love yourself. Though these commandments are distinct, they also are inseparable. We cannot truly love God unless we love our neighbor. When we practice mercy, compassion, and humility, we honor God by caring for God's children. These are meant to be the rhythm of our lives as we seek for God.

John's Baptism

Having heard John's message to the crowds who came to see him, let's consider the act he is best known for, baptism.

John and his disciples baptized multitudes of people in the wilderness of Judea. It is here that he baptized Jesus. Among the most moving experiences when I lead people on trips to the Holy Land is remembering our baptisms in the Jordan River, and even more moving are the times when I am able to baptize someone who has never been baptized, in the river where John baptized Jesus.

There are two primary locations where those visiting the Holy Land remember their baptisms. One is Yardenit, just south of the Sea of Galilee. It is beautiful, the water is clear, and it is easily accessible. For years this was where travelers to Israel went to remember their baptisms, and many still do. It is beautiful, but not likely anywhere near where John baptized. That doesn't take away from the experience of recalling one's baptism in the Jordan, but if you are wanting to get a sense of where John was baptizing, there is another location, sixty miles south of the Yardenit, that is likely to be closer to the place John baptized and which gives a better sense of the experience of Jesus when he was baptized.

This site is about five miles north of the Dead Sea and is actually two sites, one on either side of the Jordan River. On the west side of the Jordan, and most easily accessible to those visiting Israel, is Qasr al Yahud, opened in 2011. On the opposite side of the river in Jordan, and a more extensive site, is Al-Maghtas (which means, "place of baptism").

This is also known as Bethany Beyond Jordan, after the location referred to in John 1:28, where John was said to be baptizing. Israeli soldiers stand at Qasr al Yahud while Jordanian solders stand fifty yards away, on the Jordanian side of the riverbank. Both sites have facilities for visitors to purchase baptismal gowns and towels; there are changing rooms and showers to allow for baptismal remembrance or baptism in the Jordan.

Since at least the fourth century, Al-Maghtas on the Jordanian side has been the site of pilgrims remembering John's baptism of Jesus, as well as their own baptisms. There are ruins of ancient churches, what appears to be the original site of baptismal remembrance, and hermit caves where monastics came to pray. Nearby is a hill associated with the place where Elijah ascended to heaven in a chariot of fire. This site is also associated with the location where the Israelites crossed into the Promised Land under Joshua more than 1,200 years before the time of John and Jesus. A new Greek Orthodox church has been constructed with plans for as many as twelve other churches in the years ahead. But getting to the site in Jordan requires advance planning and, consequently, far fewer make the journey to it. You can find out more by visiting baptismsite.com.

The first time I visited the site at Qasr al Yahud, the Israeli army was still clearing mines from the fields around

The Jordan River at Qasr al Yahud.

the site. I was there with only a guide and a film crew and there was no one else around. I was surprised by how relatively narrow the Jordan is at this location. I'd guess perhaps fifty feet or less across. Tall reeds grow up on either side. Unlike the clear water that flows out of the Sea of Galilee at Yardenit, here the water is a milky gray, not from pollution, but from the 120 miles of clay riverbed the water runs through as the Jordan winds back and forth from Yardenit to Qasr al Yahud. I remember wading into the Jordan trying to lodge in my brain every feeling, what I saw and felt, as I stepped into the water.

It was March and I was struck, first, by how cold the water was. I had to catch my breath as I stepped into the water. But what really stood out to me was the feeling of my feet sinking into the soft clay of the riverbed. I'd worn sandals not sure whether it was rocky under the surface, but my sandals were immediately stuck in the clay, and the next step was barefoot with the mud oozing between my toes. It may seem odd, but I laughed as I thought that this wonderfully squishy feeling between my toes was likely what Jesus experienced as he stepped into the river to be baptized by his cousin.

Wading several feet off the shore, the water was now chest high, and I stopped and looked around. There was a white bird flying overhead, a dove or perhaps an egret, but a reminder for me of the Holy Spirit descending upon Jesus on the day of his baptism. I immersed myself in the water praying, "Lord, I come to this place where you were baptized by John to remember my baptism. As I do, I repent of my sin. I want to follow you, to be wholly yours. Wash me by your grace, and fill me anew with your Holy Spirit as I renew my baptismal covenant with you."

It was a meaningful experience for me as it was for the many people I've taken there since to renew their own baptisms. Each time I'm there, I try to imagine John standing near the water's edge, or perhaps wading in the water himself, preaching, calling people to repent and to bear fruit worthy of repentance. I picture the crowds standing there, having journeyed for hours. (It is a two-hour walk to Jericho, the largest nearby city, and an eight-hour walk from Jerusalem at a normal stroll. For those who came from the Galilee, as Jesus did, it was a three- to six-day journey, if not more.) What drew them there? What were they feeling inside that motivated them to make this journey? What were they hoping for?

When I read this story in scripture I'm reminded of the scene in the 2000 film, *O Brother Where Art Thou* when three escaped convicts stumble upon a baptismal service at a river. The film is loosely based upon Homer's *Odyssey*, but the baptismal scene captures the longing we sometimes have for grace and to be washed clean. In it, two of the convicts run into the river, anxious to be cleansed of their sins and born anew. The Cohen Brothers masterfully underscored this scene with an old gospel hymn from the 1800s, hauntingly recorded by Alison Krauss, *Down in the River to Pray*. Listen to the song if you get a chance, or better yet, watch the scene from the film—you can find it online.

I wonder if any of those who had walked for hours to hear John, and to wade into the water, felt the same longing for redemption that Pete and Delmar, the convicts in the film, felt. I wonder if you've ever felt that—a nearly desperate need to know that God had forgiven you after you had made a mess of your life? And if you have, you can understand how John's preaching and call to baptism was preparing the way for the Lord in the lives of his hearers.

As the water washed over those John baptized, the symbolic value of this was powerful and varied. There was the obvious imagery of being washed, cleansed, and having one's sins carried away. But as with Christian baptism, there was also the imagery of death and resurrection, dying to the old self and being resurrected as a new person. There was the imagery of birth—we are surrounded by water in the womb, and through water we are born into this world. The waters of baptism came to be seen by early Christians as the womb of God. There was liberation implied as those coming to be baptized joined in the act of passing through the waters of the Red Sea as they were liberated from slavery in Egypt, and passed through the Jordan at nearly that same spot where their forebearers entered the Promised Land.

But it was the idea of forgiveness, cleansing and starting anew (changing their minds and hearts) that seemed most clear in John's preaching and the crowd's response. And here the prophet whose name meant "Yahweh is Gracious" was inviting them into the water to accept the grace of God.

When Jesus and his followers continued this practice of baptizing, it came to signify both repentance and forgiveness, but also much more. It came to be a rite of initiation into the Christian faith, a sign of the new covenant, serving much the same role that circumcision played in Judaism. As Christians remembered God's word to Jesus in his baptism, "this is my beloved Son," they saw baptism as an expression of God's adoption of the one being baptized as God's beloved child. They saw in the water of baptism death and resurrection, a drowning to sin and being resurrected as a new creation in Christ. As they remembered Jesus's words about being "born of water and the Spirit" they saw in the baptismal waters the "womb of God" by which they were born anew. They remembered the descent of the Spirit on Jesus as he was baptized, and came to pray for the Spirit to descend on all who are baptized. Christians came to see this act of baptism as a sign of God's gracious work in those being baptized.

Christians came to see this act of baptism as a sign of God's gracious work in those being baptized.

There is so much more that could be said of Christian baptism. Each denomination has nuanced ways of looking at this powerful act. I've only scratched the surface. But notice that it was, for John, an act of preparing the way for the Lord, beckoning people to repentance and washing, by which the one being baptized sought God's forgiveness and pledged to "bear fruit worthy of repentance."

On each subsequent visit to the baptismal site on the Jordan River, I've taken groups with me there. The night before I prepare our people for the experience. For those who have never been baptized, but are desiring to do so, we have a special meeting together to discuss the meaning of baptism. I let everyone know that if they wish to be baptized, or if they have been baptized previously, if they wish to reaffirm their baptismal vows, there are two options. If they don't wish to get in the water and be immersed, they can plan to take off their shoes and socks and simply step down the steps into the river until their feet are immersed. I or one of the pastors with me will pour water upon their head or, for those who have already been baptized, make the sign of the cross on their forehead with the water. But if they wish to be immersed in the Jordan, I explain that they will need to wear clothing that can get wet, bring a bag to place their wet garments in, and have a change of clothes. They need to wear swimsuits or other appropriate clothes as the white robes available for purchase are sheer when wet and appropriate clothing underneath is important. The gift

A service of baptismal remembrance at the Jordan River.

shop at the site sells robes and towels, and as I noted above, has showers and changing rooms.

Upon arrival and after everyone has changed, we'll recount the story of John the Baptist's ministry and his baptism of Jesus. Then I'll invite those with me to ponder for a few minutes what they need to repent of, and what sins they would silently confess to God, giving them time to do just that (remember, Matthew noted the people came confessing their sins to God as they were preparing to be baptized by John). Then I'll ask the group questions appropriate for the reaffirmation of baptismal vows and questions for those being baptized. Then we'll baptize those who have never been baptized and reaffirm the vows of those who have. It is a powerful moment in which each person repents, accepts God's grace, and offers themselves to God.

In Advent we prepare to rightly celebrate once more the coming of Christ, and ready ourselves for his return. This would be a great time for you to renew your baptismal covenant, or, if you've never been baptized, to be baptized as an expression of your need for God's grace, your desire to follow Christ, and your yearning for God to pour out his Spirit upon you. Speak to your pastor about being baptized or renewing your baptism. If you are studying this book with a group, invite your pastor to renew the vows of all in your group at one time. If you are a pastor, and you are preaching through this book, plan to include a renewal of baptismal vows in your service.

But it does not require a special service to remember one's baptism, your repentance and pledge to God, and God's grace, mercy, and promises to you. In most Catholic churches there is holy water at the entrance to the sanctuary. Catholics will dip their finger in the water, make the sign of the cross on their forehead, and remember their baptism. At Church of the Resurrection, we have water by each major entrance to our sanctuary where people can pause to remember their baptism every time they walk into or out of the building. I do this every time I walk past these beautiful water features.

Some years ago, I invited our members to remember their baptism each morning as they enter the shower or bath, and in doing so, to once again receive God's grace and to yield themselves once more to God. We created a plastic prayer card that hangs in their shower with this prayer:

> Lord, as I enter the water to bathe, I remember my baptism. Wash me by your grace. Fill me with your Spirit. Renew my soul. Help me to live as your child today, and honor you in all that I do.

Every morning as I start my day I pray that prayer, a reminder of my baptism, my identity as a child of God, and my pledge to be follower of Christ.

John invited people to make a fundamental change in their hearts and minds, repenting of their sins, yielding their lives to God, and receiving his grace. They were doing this preparing the way for the Lord to work in their lives, and through them to impact the world. Every morning as I step into the shower and pray, I am doing the same thing, though as a Christian, I am remembering God's grace, confessing my sins, inviting God to wash me, and inviting the Spirit to fill me as I seek to follow Christ in my life that day.

You don't have to go to Israel or Jordan to remember your baptism and to renew your covenant. You can do it each day in your shower. You can do it at your church's baptismal font. You can do it right now as you pray,

Lord, forgive me, wash me, fill me. I offer myself to you and renew once more the promise made at my baptism. I confess you, Jesus, as my Savior and my Lord. Help me to follow you today and honor you in all that I do.

4

WITNESSES, TESTIFYING TO THE LIGHT

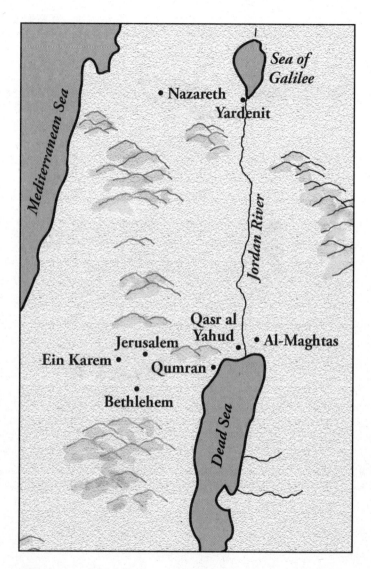

4

WITNESSES, TESTIFYING TO THE LIGHT

In the beginning was the Word
and the Word was with God
and the Word was God.
The Word was with God in the beginning.
Everything came into being through the Word,
and without the Word
nothing came into being.
What came into being
through the Word was life,
and the life was the light for all people.
The light shines in the darkness,
and the darkness doesn't extinguish the light.

A man named John was sent from God. He came as a witness to testify concerning the light, so that through him everyone would believe in the light. He himself wasn't the light, but his mission was to testify concerning the light.

The true light that shines on all people
was coming into the world....

The Word became flesh
and made his home among us.

John 1:1-9, 14a

In the last chapter we looked at John's message and the meaning of his baptism. In this chapter we'll look at the relationship between John and Jesus. We'll consider the tension between John's disciples and Jesus's disciples, and we'll look at John's death. Then we'll turn to the Gospel of John where we find in John a model for how we live our lives. Let's begin with the relationship between John and Jesus.

John and Jesus

In all four Gospels, Jesus's public ministry begins with his baptism by John in the Jordan.

Without Luke's Gospel, we might assume Jesus's baptism was their first meeting. But in Luke we learned that Elizabeth and Mary were close relatives, so close that when Mary learned she was pregnant, she traveled more than a week to find her cousin or aunt, Elizabeth. Mary stayed with Elizabeth for the last three months of Elizabeth's pregnancy with John, which corresponded to the first three months of Mary's pregnancy. These women clearly had a special bond. It seems likely that John and Jesus, cousins, would have shared a similar bond growing up.

While John lived near Jerusalem, and Jesus lived in the Galilee, Luke tells us that Joseph, Mary, and Jesus made it their custom to travel to Jerusalem for the Jewish religious festivals. There were three festivals that Jews were likely to attend in the Holy City: the pilgrimage festivals of Passover, Pentecost (Shavuot), and Booths (Sukkot). Jews would typically remain in Jerusalem or the surrounding area for a week at each festival. It makes sense that during these festivals, the cousins, John and Jesus, would have spent time together in John's hometown of Ein Karem or in Jerusalem.

As I noted in the last chapter, many believe John spent time as a part of the community of Essene monastics living at Qumran on the northwest shore of the Dead Sea. There were also Essenes living in Jerusalem. If John and Jesus grew up spending time with one another at the festivals, it is also likely that Jesus visited John at Qumran. And whether he did or didn't, if they spent time with one another in their teens and twenties, they surely spent hours discussing scripture, theology, ethics, the coming of the Messiah, and more.

I mention this because scholars who have studied the Dead Sea Scrolls note not only the similarities between the theology and practices found in the Dead Sea Scrolls and John's life and message but also between the scrolls and the teachings and ministry of Jesus. There are significant connections here that point to Jesus's awareness of, and engagement with, the ideas of the community of the Dead Sea Scrolls.

The Dead Sea Scrolls we have were largely written before the birth of Jesus. Of the one thousand scrolls or partial scrolls found, a quarter are copies of scrolls from the Hebrew Bible (the Christian Old Testament). Another group are commentaries on the biblical material. But many of the remaining scrolls describe the beliefs and practices of the community who produced them. The scrolls point to their hopes and beliefs concerning the coming of the Messiah, their thinking about the final battle between good and evil, the frustrations with the religious authorities in Jerusalem, and the Essenes' rule for community life.

The apparent founder of the Essenes, or at least the community at Qumran, was called, "the Teacher of Righteousness," who some believe was the high priest in Jerusalem until he was forced out in 152 BC. Some have found in the writings about him a figure that foreshadowed Jesus, though the Teacher was himself awaiting the coming of the Messiah while Jesus was the Messiah.

There are glimpses of the ideas found in the Dead Sea Scrolls in Jesus's life, teachings, and ministry. In these we may find the influence of John the Baptist on Jesus as they were in their teens and twenties in conversation with one another.

The idea that Jesus was influenced by the Essenes, and by John the Baptist, seems odd to some Christians. We tend to imagine that, even as an infant, Jesus fully understood his identity and God's plans, and that he was completely omniscient. If that was so, Jesus of course would not have been influenced or shaped by John. But that does not seem to be consistent with the idea that Jesus was, as the Chalcedonian Creed of 451 notes, both "truly God and truly man" and "in all things like unto us except without sin." To be human is to be born needing to learn, to grow, to mature. That is part of the human experience. Jesus had to learn to talk, to walk, to read. And he seems to have grown in his self-understanding, his understanding of his relationship to God, and the Kingdom he sought to champion.

In Philippians 2:7, Paul notes that Christ "emptied himself" by "becoming like human beings." Paul seems to have implied that Christ freely set aside those attributes of deity like omniscience, in order to walk in our shoes as a mortal. For these reasons we can speak about Jesus's own theology and self-understanding evolving and growing from the time he was born until his baptism by John when God spoke and said, "You are my beloved Son."

Jesus's and John's births were both the result of a special conception. They were both dedicated to God before they were born. God called both to play a pivotal role in God's plans. They both called people to repentance and baptism. They both announced the kingdom of God was near. John knew he was the forerunner, preparing the way for the Messiah. Jesus and John both believed Jesus was that Messiah.

Matthew describes the moment when Jesus came to be baptized in this way:

> *At that time Jesus came from Galilee to the Jordan River so that John would baptize him. John tried to stop him and said, "I need to be baptized by you, yet you come to me?"*
>
> *Jesus answered, "Allow me to be baptized now. This is necessary to fulfill all righteousness."*
>
> *So John agreed to baptize Jesus.*
>
> *(Matthew 3:13-15)*

John had been preaching for several months when Jesus arrived. Their short conversation as Jesus arrived suggest that they knew one another well, and that John saw Jesus as "one greater than I." In Matthew's account of the baptism, John recognizes that Jesus should be baptizing him, not the other way around.

It is also possible that Jesus's baptism served as a kind of ordination and initial anointing for him.

Some have asked why Jesus needed to be baptized at all. He had not sinned, why would he need a baptism of repentance for the forgiveness of sins? The answer may be that *the baptism wasn't for him, but for us.* In it he identified with us and our human condition. He also set an example for all who would follow him. But it is also possible that Jesus's baptism served as a kind of ordination and initial anointing for him. In it he yields himself to his Father, the Holy Spirit comes upon him, and he hears God's voice testifying, "This is my Son whom I dearly love." Jesus's baptism by John, at least in Matthew, Mark, and Luke, marks the beginning of his ministry.

"He Must Increase and I Must Decrease"

As John began to preach and baptize, word about him spread rapidly. People came from all over to be baptized by him. Though he may have ministered publicly for only a year or two before he was put to death, as we will see, those who were baptized by him spread across the Roman Empire. He did prepare the way for the Lord.

John had disciples. Some of John's disciples eventually left him to follow Jesus, as we read in John 1:35-37, "The next day John was standing again with two of his disciples. When he saw Jesus walking along he said, 'Look! The Lamb of God!' The two disciples heard what he said, and they followed Jesus." One of these two disciples was Andrew, Simon Peter's brother. But even as Jesus called disciples and began his public ministry, John continued to have disciples who followed him and assisted in his ministry so that there were two complementary movements taking place, led by each of these cousins.

There were some differences that became clear between John and the life he lived and called his disciples to, and

Jesus and the life he lived and called his disciples to. Jesus began preaching a very similar message to John's: "Repent for the kingdom of God is at hand." Jesus and his disciples began their ministry baptizing as John and his disciples did. But their ministry soon saw subtle and sometimes more significant differences emerge.

John's message as recorded in the Gospels could seem a bit harsh and direct, while Jesus's harsh words were reserved for the religious leaders. For ordinary sinners, Jesus spoke with compassion and mercy. John remained in the wilderness. Jesus moved about the towns and villages. John focused on baptism, while Jesus devoted much of his ministry to healing and deliverance. John continued to live the life of an ascetic, fasting and praying. Jesus also fasted and prayed, but he and his disciples often shared meals with others so that his critics called him a glutton and drunkard (Matthew 11:19 and Luke 7:34).

Others noticed the differences between their two ministries. In Luke 5:33 we read, "Some people said to Jesus, 'The disciples of John fast often and pray frequently. The disciples of the Pharisees do the same, but your disciples are always eating and drinking.'"

At one point John began to have questions as to whether Jesus really was the Messiah whom he'd been preparing the way for. In Luke 7:18-19 we read, "John called two of his disciples and sent them to the Lord. They were to ask him, 'Are you the one who is coming, or should we look for someone else?'"

In response Jesus healed a number of people who were in the crowd, then said to John's disciples, "Go, report to John what you have seen and heard. Those who were blind are able to see. Those who were crippled now walk. People with skin diseases are cleansed. Those who were deaf now hear. Those who were dead are raised up. And good news is preached to the poor" (7:22). Jesus was alluding to the promises made by God in Isaiah that he was fulfilling,

> *Then the eyes of the blind will be opened,*
> *and the ears of the deaf will be cleared.*
> *Then the lame will leap like the deer,*
> *and the tongue of the speechless will sing.*
> *(Isaiah 35:5-6a)*

> *The LORD God's spirit is upon me,*
> *because the LORD has anointed me.*
> *He has sent me*
> *to bring good news to the poor.*
> *(Isaiah 61:1)*

At one point John's disciples appear concerned about Jesus's popularity. In John 3:26 we read that John's disciples approached him and said, "Rabbi, look! The man who was with you across the Jordan, the one about whom you testified, is baptizing and everyone is flocking to him." We'll consider John's response below.

Following Jesus's death and resurrection, his disciples took his message across the Roman world and beyond. But we know that John's movement and his disciples continued his work in some form as well. And it seems, at times, that there was some confusion, or even friction, between the two movements.

We see a bit of this confusion in two stories in Acts 18 and 19, both occurring twenty-five years after the death of John the Baptist. In Acts 18:25, a man named Apollos shows up in Ephesus, and it was said that he "he taught accurately the things about Jesus, even though he was aware only of the baptism John proclaimed and practiced." Priscilla and Aquila, two disciples of Jesus that Paul had mentored, "explained to him God's way more accurately" (verse 26). In Acts 19:1-5, we find a group of disciples who seem to have believed something about Jesus, but who were baptized with John's baptism (by John, or by his disciples):

> *While Apollos was in Corinth, Paul took a route through the interior and came to Ephesus, where he found some disciples. He asked them, "Did you receive the Holy Spirit when you came to believe?"*

115

They replied, "We've not even heard that there is a Holy Spirit."

Then he said, "What baptism did you receive, then?"

They answered, "John's baptism."

Paul explained, "John baptized with a baptism by which people showed they were changing their hearts and lives. It was a baptism that told people about the one who was coming after him. This is the one in whom they were to believe. This one is Jesus." After they listened to Paul, they were baptized in the name of the Lord Jesus.

The Gospels were written at various times between perhaps AD 65 and 85. John died around AD 30. Many scholars believe that John's disciples were still active at the time the Gospels were written and that at least some of what we read about John in the Gospels was aimed at bringing these two groups together. The Gospels honor John, while reminding readers of John's words about Jesus.

We see this in Mark, our earliest Gospel, written at least thirty-five years after John died. There John says, "One stronger than I am is coming after me. I'm not even worthy to bend over and loosen the strap of his sandals. I baptize you with water, but he will baptize you with the Holy Spirit" (Mark 1:7-8). John is reported to have said similar things by Matthew and Luke.

We see this concern, to honor John the Baptist but also to make clear that Jesus, not John, was the Messiah, particularly pronounced in the Gospel According to John (the Gospel traditionally ascribed to Jesus's disciple, John, not John the Baptist). In John 1:6-8 we read, "A man named John was sent from God. He came as a witness to testify concerning the light, so that through him everyone would believe in the light. *He himself wasn't the light*, but his mission was to testify concerning the light" (emphasis added here and in the passages below). We'll come back to this text at the end of the chapter, but here we can see that John the Gospel writer is seeking to clarify that John was not the light, but a witness to the light.

Again, in John 1:15, "John testified about him, crying out, 'This is the one of whom I said, '*He who comes after me is greater than me because he existed before me.*'" And in John 1:19-20 we read, "This is John's testimony when the Jewish leaders in Jerusalem sent priests and Levites to ask him, 'Who are you?' John confessed (he didn't deny but confessed), '*I'm not the Christ.*'" That episode concludes with familiar words from the other Gospels as John says, "I baptize with water. *Someone greater stands among you*, whom you don't recognize. He comes after me, but *I'm not worthy to untie his sandal straps*" (verses 26-27). And finally, John 1 ends with John the Baptist revealing who Jesus is:

"The next day John saw Jesus coming toward him and said, "Look! *The Lamb of God* who takes away the sin of the world! This is the one about whom I said, '*He who comes after me is really greater than me because he existed before me*'" (John 1:29-30). And just after this John the Baptist notes, "*I have seen and testified that this one is God's Son*" (verse 34). Why the repeated emphasis on John's supporting role for Jesus's ministry, and Jesus's identity as the light, the lamb, the preexistent Son of God? It seems to be a way of reaching out to John's followers, while also making clear that Jesus was the Messiah John proclaimed.

As an aside, there exists a religion called Mandaeism (and sometimes Sabianism), with about sixty thousand adherents around the world, that considers John the Baptist, not Jesus, to be their chief prophet. They live near rivers or streams and continue to practice regular ritual bathing. They may have originated from some of the original followers of John, though the theology and writings of the religion seem heavily influenced by Gnosticism.

All of this is interesting, but there is a point here I don't want you to miss, one by which John the Baptist continues to help us in preparing the way for the Lord in our lives.

Let's return to the passage in John 3:27-30, where John's disciples came to him concerned that Jesus had large crowds flocking to him. Listen to John's reply,

John replied, "No one can receive anything unless it is given from heaven. You yourselves can testify that I said that I'm not the Christ but that I'm the one sent before him. The groom is the one who is getting married. The friend of the groom stands close by and, when he hears him, is overjoyed at the groom's voice. Therefore, my joy is now complete. He must increase and I must decrease.

John was a driven, passionate man who loved God and longed to play his part in preparing the way for the Lord, and for the kingdom of God. He was a leader who had a clear vision and the capacity to inspire people. In a very short period of time, he had developed renown across the entirety of the Holy Land. He'd gained the attention of the religious leaders in Jerusalem and Herod Antipas who ruled the Galilee and the region on the east side of the Jordan where John was baptizing. He was determined, charismatic, visionary, passionate, committed... and humble.

When Jesus, his slightly younger cousin came along to be baptized, John felt confident that Jesus was the one to lead the revolution John was preaching. John knew the movement he had started was not about him. He kept pointing to Jesus, testifying to him, seeking to prepare people to be a part of the Kingdom that Jesus proclaimed. People thought he might be the Messiah, but he constantly said that he was not the one, but one greater than he was

119

coming. He was nearly universally respected and admired, yet he was glad to point his disciples to Jesus. He took genuine joy when Jesus's ministry began to flourish. And I particularly love this line, *He must increase and I must decrease.*

He must increase and I must decrease.

I am reminded of what Jim Collins says about leaders in his best-selling book, *Good to Great.* He speaks about the kind of leaders that move a company from good to great. He calls them, "level 5 leaders." Collins tells story after story in the book and in articles he's written about these kinds of leaders. They all demonstrate two qualities that they hold in tension: They have "extreme personal humility" and "intense professional will." Collins noted, "Level 5 leaders are a study in duality: modest and willful, humble and fearless."[1] Their focus is not on their personal ambition or accomplishments or meeting their ego needs, but they are relentless in their pursuit of what is good for their organization, customers, and employees; their ambition is for their organization's mission and vision.

This is the kind of leadership and character we see in both John and Jesus. It is why John celebrated Jesus's success and could also say that "he must increase and I must decrease." It is also why Jesus could wash his disciples' feet at the Last Supper and teach them that the "truly great among you will be your servant." It is why both were willing to die for their mission and calling.

Pastors are human. I recall some years ago speaking with a young pastor who was doing creative and innovative things leading the United Methodist church he was pastoring. The congregation was growing rapidly. Despite this success, he told me he had felt isolated and rejected by some of his colleagues in neighboring United Methodist churches. But that was beginning to change. He told me that recently one of his colleagues came to him and said,

> "I want to apologize to you. I've said unkind things about you that I've come to realize were not true. I struggled with your success as I felt like it was an indication that I was a failure. I felt better, for a little while, if I said unkind things about you, but the lift only lasted a little while. Then I felt worse—embarrassed and ashamed. I realized this was not about you, but about my insecurities. Then it hit me, we're on the same team. We're both trying to help people know Jesus, to follow him, to grow in him and to live

their faith in the world. Since then, I've been
thanking God for you, and asking how I can
learn from you. I feel better about myself, and
I feel grateful for you."

I knew a pastor who was approaching the last ten years
of his ministry. He began to make this his mantra: "Others
must increase, and I must decrease." He began pouring
into the lives and leadership of other pastors, encouraging
them and mentoring them. He knew that this statement
was literally true for him. In preparing for a transition in
his life and ministry, and readying the church he served for
the future, he had to decrease and others in leadership had
to increase.

Finally, these words of John the Baptist are actually a
profound prayer and vision for the Christian spiritual life.
John was speaking these words about Jesus when he said,
"He must increase and I must decrease." What if this was
our goal? The spirit of this idea is captured in a short prayer
you may have prayed before, "More of Thee and less of me."
The idea is simple yet profound. In my life, I want the focus
of my will, my thinking, my speaking, my living to be more
about Christ than it is on me.

I spoke this morning with a friend of mine, who last
year was diagnosed with early onset Parkinson's disease. It
was a devastating blow. But since the diagnosis, he's had

great medical care, he's exercising, and he's doing great. One thing he told me was that each morning he prays the Wesley Covenant Prayer. I've shared this prayer in many of my books. John Wesley, Methodism's founder, adapted this prayer from a Puritan named Richard Alleine who first composed a version of it in 1663. The prayer captures this idea of More of Thee and less of me, or He must increase and I must decrease. Like my friend, I pray some version of this prayer, sometimes abbreviated to, "Here I am Lord, do with me whatever you want," every morning. I'd invite you to pause and to pray the prayer now. Here are its words,

> I am no longer my own, but thine.
> Put me to what thou wilt, rank me with whom
> thou wilt.
> Put me to doing, put me to suffering.
> Let me be employed by thee or laid aside for thee,
> exalted for thee or brought low for thee.
> Let me be full, let me be empty.
> Let me have all things, let me have nothing.
> I freely and heartily yield all things
> to thy pleasure and disposal.
> And now, O glorious and blessed God,
> Father, Son, and Holy Spirit,
> thou art mine, and I am thine. So be it.
> And the covenant which I have made on earth,
> let it be ratified in heaven. Amen.[2]

John's Arrest and Death

We turn now to John's death. As we have learned, in a short period of time, John's ministry was the talk of people across the Holy Land. Herod Antipas, the son of King Herod the Great, had heard of John. Antipas ruled over the Galilee and Perea, the region on the east bank of the Jordan. When John baptized in Aenon and Bethany, he was baptizing in Perea, Herod Antipas's territory.

The story of John's death at the hands of Herod Antipas, likely a year or two after he began his public ministry, is as fascinating as it is tragic. Both Mark 6:14-29 and Matthew 14:3-12 tell the story. Josephus, the first-century Jewish historian, also tells of John's death, though a slightly different version of the story.

Matthew, Mark, and Josephus all agree that Herod Antipas had fallen in love with Herodias, the wife of his half-brother, Herod Philip. Herodias agreed to divorce Philip. Antipas agreed to divorce his wife, Phasaelis, the daughter of King Aretas IV of Nabatea. Soon Herod Antipas and Herodias married. Interestingly, Herodias was not only Antipas's brother's ex-wife, she was also Antipas's niece. That sounds like a modern soap opera. John the Baptist spoke out against this marriage and publicly denounced Herod Antipas and Herodias as sinful. In response, Herod locked John up in prison at his palace near Jericho, not far from where John had been baptizing.

Here's how Mark tells the story of John's arrest:

Herod himself had arranged to have John arrested and put in prison because of Herodias, the wife of Herod's brother Philip. Herod had married her, but John told Herod, "It's against the law for you to marry your brother's wife!" So Herodias had it in for John. She wanted to kill him, but she couldn't. This was because Herod respected John. He regarded him as a righteous and holy person, so he protected him. John's words greatly confused Herod, yet he enjoyed listening to him.

(Mark 6:17-20)

Some would call John's preaching mixing religion and politics. But John was inviting people to repent and expected Herod Antipas, who ruled as Tetrarch, if he were to rule over the Jews, to seek to live like one. It took great courage to speak up.

While John was Herod Antipas's prisoner, Herod actually listened to John, came to respect him, saw him as righteous and holy, and sought to protect him. This tells us something about John and how he must have spoken to Herod while in prison. John called him to repentance, but in a way that garnered the respect of Herod.

Herodias, however, was not impressed. So here's what happened next. At a dinner party celebrating Herod's birthday, Herodias's daughter danced for the king and his dinner guests. Afterwards he said, "Ask me for whatever you want, up to half of my kingdom!" She asked Herodias what she should ask for, and her mother said, "Ask for the head of John the Baptist."

> *Hurrying back to the ruler, she made her request: "I want you to give me John the Baptist's head on a plate, right this minute." Although the king was upset, because of his solemn pledge and his guests, he didn't want to refuse her. So he ordered a guard to bring John's head. The guard went to the prison, cut off John's head, brought his head on a plate, and gave it to the young woman, and she gave it to her mother. When John's disciples heard what had happened, they came and took his dead body and laid it in a tomb.*
>
> (Mark 6:25-29)

John reflected courage in speaking truth to power. He had called out behavior the Law of Moses forbade (see Leviticus 18:16 and 20:21). Herod Antipas displayed injustice and cowardice in not refusing Herodias's daughter's request. And once more we see how power can corrupt and be misused.

I made the final revisions to this book as Russian President Vladimir Putin ordered his army to invade Ukraine under false pretenses. It seemed unthinkable that a major world power would send nearly two hundred thousand troops, tanks, and other heavy artillery into battle against a neighbor, unprovoked. Thousands, at this point, have died. Cities have been flattened. By the time you read this, you the reader may know how this war was resolved, but as I write, it is difficult to see a way out.

Evil, injustice, cruelty, and inhumanity never ultimately prevail.

What I do know is that evil, injustice, cruelty, and inhumanity never ultimately prevail. Putin launched his war, in part, to prevent Ukraine and other neighboring countries from joining NATO. But instead he's moved countries that might not have planned to join NATO to seriously consider doing so. He sought to win a quick victory and impose Russia's will on Ukraine and other countries. Instead he brought an economic disaster on his own country and alienated much of the world. We know that the abuse and misuse of power does not engender love and loyalty. This approach may silence one's opponents for a time, but it only makes the bully a pariah in the end. One way or another, justice ultimately prevails.

By the way, Herod Antipas, who had John beheaded, would later meet Jesus, on Good Friday while he was in Jerusalem. Pontius Pilate had interrogated Jesus after he was charged with insurrection by the religious leaders. Finding that Jesus was from the Galilee, Herod Antipas's jurisdiction, and knowing that Antipas was in Jerusalem for the Passover, he sent Jesus to Herod for a decision on whether to put Jesus to death. Though Herod found no basis for putting Jesus to death, and could have set him free, he mocked Jesus, dressed him in a royal robe, and sent him back to Pilate. Within an hour or two, Jesus was crucified.

What eventually happened to Herod Antipas? King Aretas IV, the Nabatean king and father of Antipas's first wife, waged a war against Herod in response to his divorcing her. He crushed Herod's army. Josephus, the first-century Jewish historian, tells us that those in Herod's realm believed "the destruction of Herod's army came from God...as a just punishment of what Herod had done against John, who was called the Baptist."[3]

Here's the question John's death brings to my mind, for me, and now for you: What am I willing to die for? I am reminded of the forty-four-year-old Ukrainian president, when the US offered to safely evacuate him from Kyiv saying, "I need ammunition, not a ride." He was prepared to die for what he believed in. Zelensky is not John nor

Jesus, but they, too, were willing to die in pursuit of their mission.

In the introduction of this book, I mentioned a prayer from The United Methodist "Service of Death and Resurrection." I wonder if you might actually pause to pray that prayer with me now:

> Help us to live as those who are prepared to die.
> And when our days here are accomplished,
>> enable us to die as those who go forth to live,
>> so that living or dying, our life may be in you,
>> and that nothing in life or in death will be
>> able to separate us from your great love in
>> Christ Jesus our Lord.[4]

Not the Light, but Testifying to the Light

Most of what we've learned about John the Baptist has been from what are called the "Synoptic Gospels," Matthew, Mark, and Luke. *Synoptic*, as you likely know, means "to see together," and these three are called the Synoptic Gospels because they tell the story of Jesus in very similar ways and share many of the same stories and details. As we've seen, Luke alone holds the infancy narratives of Jesus and John the Baptist. And he does not go into the detail regarding

John's death that Matthew and Mark do. Still, they tell much the same story about John the Baptist. As we close our study of John the Baptist, we'll turn to the Gospel of John, which gives us a different view of the prophet.

Like all four of the Gospels, the Gospel of John itself does not tell us who wrote it, except the cryptic phrase near the end citing "the beloved disciple" (John 21:20-24). But tradition identifies the author of this Gospel as John, the son of Zebedee, one of the twelve disciples. Clement of Alexandria, writing in the second century, famously described the Gospel of John as "the spiritual Gospel," recognizing that it tells the story of Jesus in ways that do not always align with the Synoptic Gospels, but which seem intentionally written to draw out the spiritual meaning of the events the Gospel describes, and of the significance of Jesus, and as we will see, John the Baptist.

John's Gospel was likely the last Gospel written, and it has the most highly developed Christology (the understanding of the identity and work of Jesus) found anywhere in the New Testament. As we will see in a moment, the Gospel begins with a dramatic statement that speaks of Christ as the divine *logos*, the Word of God wrapped in human flesh. John's Gospel is famous for its many "I Am" statements, in which Jesus makes powerful statements about himself, with a hint at his shared identity with God whose personal name, Yahweh, means something like, "I Am." Jesus says, I Am the bread of life. I Am the light of the world. I Am the door for the sheep. I Am the good shepherd. I Am the resurrection and the life. I Am the way, the truth, and the life. And I Am the true vine.

There's so much more in John than the "I Am" statements, but they summarize the Gospel's powerful picture of who Jesus is. John's statements about Jesus prepare us for the climax of Advent as we celebrate the birth of Jesus in Bethlehem, and as we ponder Christ's return, his second advent.

On Christmas Eve, every year at the Church of the Resurrection, when we prepare to light the Christ candle and then pass the candlelight throughout the room as we sing "Silent Night," we first dim the lights, extinguish the candles, turn off the lights on the trees throughout the room. And then, in the darkness, one of our pastors reads these words from John's Gospel's majestic prologue—John's way of telling the Christmas story—as a family begins walking down the aisle, in the darkness, carrying one solitary lit candle,

> *In the beginning was the Word*
> *and the Word was with God*
> *and the Word was God.*

The Word was with God in the beginning.
Everything came into being through the Word,
    and without the Word
    nothing came into being.
What came into being
    through the Word was life,
    and the life was the light for all people.
The light shines in the darkness,
    and the darkness doesn't extinguish the light.
                                (John 1:1-5)

Then we always skip the next three verses, John 1:6-8, because they seem to be a jarring interruption, misplaced in the midst of this glorious poetry. Here are the words,

A man named John was sent from God. He came as a witness to testify concerning the light, so that through him everyone would believe in the light. He himself wasn't the light, but his mission was to testify concerning the light (emphasis added).

Why does John's Gospel insert John the Baptist right in the middle of this majestic prologue, just as it is describing Jesus as the Word of God, preexistent, present at creation, showing that he is God's character, God's essence, God's self-disclosure, the very logic of God, and the light that cannot be extinguished by darkness, bringing life to everyone?

As we've noted, some have speculated that this interruption was meant to honor John while at the same time making it clear that John was NOT the light, but his mission was to testify *to* the light. Jesus *is the light.*

Let's unpack this for a moment. I was awakened by the light of a full moon shining through my window in the middle of the night recently. It was bright enough I could see clearly my yard outside by its light. I have a telescope, a Meade LX90, that I love to take outside to look at the night sky. With my telescope and the right lens you can see the mountains on the moon, the edges of the craters, even the US flag—okay, not the flag, but amazing views of the mountains and craters! But whenever I do this, I use a lunar filter. If you don't have a lunar filter, you'll hurt your eyes if you look too long, the moon is so bright. Yet the moon doesn't produce light, it only reflects it.

This is how the Gospel of John understands the role of John the Baptist. There was something amazing happening in the birth of Jesus. God was coming to his people, to deliver, rescue, ransom, and redeem them. To make himself known to them. To show mercy and grace to them and to offer life to them. John came to testify about that light, to witness to Christ's light, to announce that the kingdom of heaven was near, that one greater than he was coming who would baptize with the Holy Spirit and with fire. He came to call people to change their hearts and their minds in preparation for the coming of the King, the Light, the Word made flesh.

This is Advent and Christmas: Jesus and John, the sun and the moon, the true light that enlightens everyone, and the one who testifies about the light.

As I write these words, I think about the darkness our world has been living through over these last few years. You may be reading this book several years after I wrote it, and you'll have your own experiences of darkness. Every year we do. But these last few years, darkness was watching a million Americans die of COVID-19 and the social isolation that the virus wrought. It was polarization over masks, school closings, and vaccines. It was watching a black man die as an officer kept a knee on his neck for nine minutes while he cried out that he could not breathe. It was more polarization in the aftermath of protests. It was political divisions that drove apart families, churches, and communities. It was school shootings and mass shootings. It was watching tanks and fighter planes attacking cities in Ukraine.

How we need the Light of Christ, the "true light that shines on all people." But Christ the light has come, two thousand years ago he came. Our task, as those who put our trust in him, is to reflect his light—to bear witness to his light. It is to live as those who have heard John's message, changing our hearts and minds, and living differently in response. It is to bear fruit worthy of repentance.

As a church, we had done that during COVID-19. I stood watching our members holding signs for hospital workers, filling cars with groceries for people who were unemployed, hosting thousands of people for vaccinations in our buildings. I witnessed it at the height of a deeply divisive election season as our members put up signs in their yards, #LOVEYOURNEIGHBORS, and then committed to random acts of kindness to express love, particularly to people of different religions or political parties or races. They were not the light, but their mission was to reflect the light.

I see it almost daily as followers of Christ are intentional about paying attention to see where they can bear witness, and reflect, the light of Christ. That's what John taught us. It is what he was inviting us to do when the crowds asked, What does it look like to repent? To prepare the way for the Lord? And he said, "Whoever has two shirts must share with the one who has none, and whoever has food must do the same."

Each year on Christmas Eve, we conclude worship at Church of the Resurrection by singing "Silent Night." By the time we're done singing, the candlelight has passed to every person in the room. We ask everyone to hold up their candlelight. The room is filled with light.

Just three minutes earlier the room was pitch dark. One small candle had come into the room, representing the baby born in Bethlehem. But as we each accepted the light, then shared the light, a miracle occurred. We filled the room with light. I always say to the crowds gathered, "Look around at all of this light! This was God's strategic plan for pushing back the darkness in the world! Christ came, and we came to believe and put our hope in him. We accept his light. Then we seek to reflect this light! And it doesn't stop here. Your candle is just a symbol of how we're meant to live. We're meant to let our light so shine before others that they may see our good works and give glory to our Father in heaven.

> *A man named John was sent from God. He came as a witness to testify concerning the light, so that through him everyone would believe in the light. He himself wasn't the light, but* his mission was to testify concerning the light.
> (John 1:6-8, emphasis added)

Not long ago, we had three hundred Afghan refugees resettle in Kansas City. They were among the Afghans who worked with American forces and whose lives were at risk as the Taliban regained control of Afghanistan. Our congregation partners with Jewish Vocational Services to help welcome these strangers in response to Jesus's words, "I was a stranger and you welcomed me." We furnish the empty homes and apartments that have been rented for the refugees. We seek to fill their new homes with the necessities for families who arrive with little more than a duffel bag. And we greet them at the airport with signs in the Pashto or Dari languages saying, "We are so glad you are here. Welcome to Kansas City!"

My wife and I and our kids and granddaughter went to the airport one night that Advent. A mom, dad, and their four children were arriving in Kansas City. The father worked for the Afghan special forces and had spent years working alongside Americans. The US government recognized the threat to him and brought him and his family to Kansas City. They arrived after dark on a stormy night. They had never been to the US and had never heard of Kansas City. They were anxious and tired.

That night in December, my wife LaVon and I, our daughter and son-in-law, Danielle and JT, and our then-seven-year-old granddaughter, Stella, stood there, holding our signs and balloons and gifts Stella had picked out for the children. And as the family arrived we sought, by our presence there, to say to them, You are not alone.

We care about you. You are welcome here. You are loved. We sought to be witnesses to the Light, and to reflect that Light to a family that had walked through the darkness.

Inviting Others to Find the Light

Many of you are reading this book as an Advent study. If you've been reading a chapter a week, you've come to the end of this book days before Christmas Eve. I want to invite you to follow John the Baptist in one more way before I close.

One of my favorite hymns was written in 1758 by a British pastor named Robert Robinson. It's called "Come Thou Fount of Every Blessing." It speaks of our tendency to wander from God, and God's relentless pursuit of us. The second verse of the hymn ends,

> Jesus sought me when a stranger,
> wandering from the fold of God;
> he, to rescue me from danger,
> bought me with his precious blood.[5]

The final verse ends with these words,

> Prone to wander, Lord I feel it
> Prone to leave the God I love
> Here's my heart, O take and seal it;
> seal it for thy courts above.

I think I feel such a connection with that hymn because it describes my experience of the Christian life. We're all prone to wander, to leave the God we love. That's true of so many people you know.

We're all prone to wander, to leave the God we love.

In 2021, it was reported that for the first time in as long as anyone could remember, the number of Americans who were members of a church dropped below 50 percent (down from 76 percent just a few decades ago). Many of those who aren't involved in church claim a faith in God, and profess to be spiritual, but not religious.

Most might actually attend a candlelight Christmas Eve service if someone they know, respect, and value would invite them. More people have come to faith or returned to faith at the Church of the Resurrection as a result of a friend inviting them to Christmas Eve services than any other time of the year.

I wonder if God is calling you to be his messenger, his witness, to prepare the way of the Lord, by inviting someone to Christmas Eve worship? Perhaps there is someone in your sphere of influence, or perhaps a host of people, that you might simply invite to join you for Christmas Eve candlelight services at your church this year. How might their lives be different if you invited and they said yes? Use your social media account to let your friends know that you'd like them to join you. Offer to sit by them when they come. Tell them what candlelight services mean to you.

We're meant to testify to the light with our actions, but also by our words in witness and invitation. Your mission, like John's, is to testify to the light.

During the 2008 presidential election campaign, Senator John McCain was asked to talk about his faith. His comments appeared in *TIME* magazine in an article entitled, "A Light Amid the Darkness." He described being a prisoner of war in Vietnam, how the guards would tie him in a painful position, with his arms behind his back and his head between his knees. They would leave him like this for long periods of time, often overnight. He then recounted one night when a guard came into his cell and loosened his ropes, giving him some relief and small comfort through the night. The guard tied the ropes back the next morning as his shift ended, without ever saying a word about what he had done.

> A month or so later, on Christmas Day, I was standing in the dirt courtyard when I saw that

same guard approach me. He walked up and stood silently next to me, not looking or smiling at me. Then he used his sandaled foot to draw a cross in the dirt. We stood wordlessly looking at the cross, remembering the true light of Christmas, even in the darkness of a Vietnamese prison camp.[6]

At that prison, a North Vietnamese prison guard testified to the light with an act of kindness and a cross drawn in the dirt. How will you testify to the light this Christmas? How will you prepare the way for the Lord?

POSTSCRIPT: JUDGMENT DAY AND THE SECOND ADVENT

The people were filled with expectation, and everyone wondered whether John might be the Christ. John replied to them all, "I baptize you with water, but the one who is more powerful than me is coming. I'm not worthy to loosen the strap of his sandals. He will baptize you with the Holy Spirit and fire. The shovel he uses to sift the wheat from the husks is in his hands. He will clean out his threshing area and bring the wheat into his barn. But he will burn the husks with a fire that can't be put out." With many other words John appealed to them, proclaiming good news to the people.

Luke 3:15-18

The Old Testament prophets understood themselves to be God's instruments calling the people to repentance—to change their minds, and hearts and actions. Long before journalists took up the idea that their task was to "comfort the afflicted and afflict the comfortable," the prophets had the job. But in a way, they weren't too different from excellent journalists.

The prophets had a keen sense of justice and they shone a light on places where it was missing. They understood geopolitics and what was happening between the great empires of their time. They knew that the only way the small kingdoms of Judah and Israel could stand, straddling the trade route coveted by the empires to the northeast and to the southwest, was by the grace of God. And if the people of that land rejected God's call for justice, and if they embraced idolatry, God's protection would be withheld from them and they would be destroyed.

The prophets routinely afflicted the comfortable with their dire warnings, yet they also comforted the afflicted with their words like we read in Isaiah 40: "Comfort, comfort my people! says your God" (40:1). They warned of things coming soon, kings and emperors on the attack. They described Israel's and Judah's destruction. But they also foretold their later restoration.

The "day of the Lord" became synonymous with a day of judgment and is mentioned by Isaiah, Ezekiel, Joel, Amos, Obadiah, Zephaniah, Zechariah, and Malachi. Malachi's closing words about the "day of the Lord" is a passage that John believed applied to him, "I am sending Elijah the prophet to you, before the great and terrifying day of the LORD arrives. Turn the hearts of the parents to the children and the hearts of the children to their parents" (Malachi 4:5-6).

John was a prophet, like the prophets of old, like Elijah after whom he patterned his dress. Like the Old Testament prophets, he warned of destruction, and like them he called people to repentance. He warned of a day of judgment that was coming, a day the Messiah would usher in: "He will baptize you with the Holy Spirit and fire. His winnowing fork is in his hand, to clear his threshing floor and to gather the wheat into his granary; but the chaff he will burn with unquenchable fire" (Luke 3:16-17 NRSV).

Repeatedly, the Hebrew prophets foretell a day when God will pour out his Spirit upon his people (see Isaiah 44:3, Ezekiel 39:29, and Joel 2:28 as examples). John uses a harvest metaphor for the final judgment as he speaks about the chaff being burned with unquenchable fire while the wheat is gathered into the granary. Again, throughout the prophets there is a repeated warning of judgment, of the day of the Lord, and often that day is described as a day when sinners will be purged with fire (see Malachi 3:1-6 as an example, a passage we've read previously in this book).

The idea of a final judgment day fits into the category of theology and biblical studies that scholars call "eschatology." Eschatology includes ideas of what happens after we die, but also of the end of history. Closely tied to eschatology is apocalyptic language—language that is rich in metaphors that reveal a future judgment, usually accompanied by the destruction of the world we live in. Both the Essenes and John, as well as Jesus, speak about the coming judgment.

I mention all of this to bring us back to where we began this book. We often think of Advent, the four weeks leading up to Christmas, as a season to spiritually prepare to celebrate anew the birth of Jesus. But Advent means coming, presence, or arrival, and the season is not only (or even primarily) a time to prepare to rightly celebrate Christmas, Christ's first coming. It is about being ready for the second advent of Christ, for the day when he returns and we will stand before his judgment seat, the day when he comes with his "winnowing fork in his hand," when the "chaff will be burned with unquenchable fire."

Many mainline Christians tend not to want to think about things like the final judgment very often. And talk about the Second Coming of Christ, while in our liturgy and lectionary scripture readings of Advent, are often over-spiritualized, so they are robbed of their power to comfort and afflict. We've done this in part as a reaction to the excessive interest in, and hyper-literal interpretation of, the Bible's eschatological and apocalyptical passages by fundamentalist Christians.

I came to faith in a wonderful Pentecostal church whose pastor, youth pastor, and people loved me and helped me to come to put my trust in Christ, and to hear God's call on my life to be a pastor. In many Pentecostal churches there is a pronounced emphasis on the Second Coming. Guest preachers would come with their charts showing how events like the re-formation of Israel as a state in 1948, the formation of the European Union, and events happening in Russia all lined up with the words of Jesus in Matthew 24, the words of Paul in 2 Thessalonians, and the visions described in the Book of Revelation. Because of the birth of the modern state of Israel in 1948, Jesus would return by 1988, many said, for forty years was a biblical generation, and Jesus said in Matthew 24:34, "I assure you that this generation won't pass away until all these things happen." Never mind that Jesus never directly mentions the re-formation of the nation of Israel, or that many of the things Jesus described in Matthew 24 already happened in AD 70 when the Temple and Jerusalem were destroyed by the Romans.

Some of you will remember books like Hal Lindsey's *The Late Great Planet Earth* or decades later, the *Left Behind* series of books or films like the 1972, *A Thief in the Night*, designed, literally, to scare the hell out of teenage kids and young adults. These were all built upon a particular way of reading the Bible's apocalyptic literature that most mainline scholars reject.

LaVon and I married the week after high school graduation in 1982, when we were seventeen and eighteen years old, in part because we'd had a steady diet of hearing how Jesus was returning soon, likely no later than 1988. Why would we wait to get married? After 1988 came and went, new dates were suggested, new interpretations given to current events, a new generation of end-times preachers speculated, and more best-selling end-times books were released.

There is not time in this short postscript to describe the various ways Christians throughout history have understood the eschatological passages in the Bible, and particularly the Book of Revelation. I have summarized this in chapter 30 of my book *Making Sense of the Bible*, (HarperOne, 2014), "Making Sense of the Book of Revelation." There I mention four ways of reading Revelation (the futurist, historicist, preterist, and idealist). Suffice it to say that most mainstream evangelical and mainline scholars do not read Revelation in the way the popular end-times-are-now folks do.

The apocalyptic and eschatological passages of scripture are words of warning and words of hope.

But that should not lead us to dismiss the idea of the second advent of Christ and the final judgment. The apocalyptic and eschatological passages of scripture are words of warning and words of hope. They warn and remind us that injustice and evil will not continue unpunished forever and that we will "appear before the judgment seat of Christ" (2 Corinthians 5:10 NRSV). They comfort us with the assurance that one day God will "wipe every tear from their eyes. Death will be no more; mourning and crying and pain will be no more" (Revelation 21:4 NRSV). The point of the warnings is for us to "stay alert! You don't know what day the Lord is coming...therefore, you also should be prepared" (Matthew 24:42 and 44).

John, Jesus, Paul, and most others in the early church seemed to believe that the "end" would come soon. The Book of Revelation closes with these words, "'Yes, I'm coming soon.' Amen. Come, Lord Jesus!" (Revelation 22:20). I don't think any of them imagined two millennia would pass before the return of Christ. Though by the time 2 Peter was written (many believe it was the last book of the New Testament written in Peter's name), the author addresses the delay in Christ's return,

> *Don't let it escape your notice, dear friends, that with the Lord a single day is like a thousand years and a thousand years are like a single day. The Lord isn't slow to keep his promise, as some think of slowness, but he is patient toward you, not wanting anyone to perish but all to change their hearts and lives. But the day of the Lord will come like a thief. On that day the heavens will pass away with a dreadful noise, the elements will be consumed by fire, and the earth and all the works done on it will be exposed.* Since everything will be destroyed in this way, what sort of people ought you to be? You must live holy and godly lives, waiting for and hastening the coming day of God.

Because of that day, the heavens will be destroyed by fire and the elements will melt away in the flames. But according to his promise we are waiting for a new heaven and a new earth, where righteousness is at home.

(2 Peter 3:8-13, emphasis added)

Second Peter then ends with this final admonition, "Grow in the grace and knowledge of our Lord and savior Jesus Christ" (3:18).

One thousand nine hundred years after Peter wrote these words, we still await the return of Christ and the "day of God." When will he return? On the one hand, it could happen at any time, perhaps even today. Are you ready? But it may be that the end won't come for another ten thousand years (or one hundred thousand years!). What is ten thousand years to God who has been overseeing our universe for fourteen billion years now. Or perhaps this talk of the final judgment was meant to be taken metaphorically, recognizing that in every generation there are cataclysmic events that claim the lives of large numbers of people and lead us to rethink our place in the world.

But, as I noted in the introduction, one thing we can be certain of—if Christ does not return in a glorious Second Coming in our lifetime, he will come back for us at our death: "When I go to prepare a place for you, *I will return* and take you to be with me so that where I am you will

151

be too" (John 14:3, emphasis added). None of us knows when our death will occur. I've officiated at hundreds of funerals. Some were elderly saints, or people who were very ill, who knew their death was imminent. But many were people who had no idea "the day or the hour" when they would die. For some, death came unexpectedly, "like a thief in the night." *The important thing is to always be prepared, to be ready to stand before the judgment seat of Christ.*

Which takes us back to John's message and the point of this book. John called us to repent—*metanoia*—to have a change of mind that leads to a change of heart that leads to a change of behavior. Where do you need to change your heart and life, knowing that "the day of the Lord" is coming? Are there patterns of thinking or values, resentments, or desires that you've allowed to take up residence in your mind that are inconsistent with God's will? It's time to repent.

Are there ways in which you you've been living, ways you speak to others, things you do in secret that need to change in your life? Are you bearing the fruit of repentance: Are you sharing your clothing and food with those in need? (Luke 3:11) Are you treating people fairly? (Luke 3:13) Are you cheating or harassing anyone? Are you content with your wages? (Luke 3:14b) Have you sought to live "holy and godly lives" and are you growing "in the grace and knowledge of our Lord and savior Jesus Christ"?

Advent is a time to repent, and to take on practices that help prepare us for the coming of the Lord. And, because we'll always fall short of the life God calls us to live, it is also a time to trust in God's grace and the promises made in our baptism, to do what we cannot do ourselves. In God's mercy God promises to wash us, to forgive us, and to make us new.

At Advent we prepare to celebrate the "good news of great joy" that Christ the Savior came to us as a babe in Bethlehem. And we remember the ministry of John, who would "go before the Lord to prepare his way." We recall that Jesus said that one day he would return for us, and we hear once again, and heed, the words of John the Baptist who, even now, helps us prepare the way for the Lord.

Lord, thank you for the life and ministry of your prophet, John the Baptist. As the multitudes did on the banks of the Jordan, so now I, too, repent of my sin. I have not done your will. I have broken your laws. I have rebelled against your love. I have not always loved my neighbors. I have not heard or responded to the cries of the needy. I am sorry. I need your grace. As you promised in my baptism, so now forgive me once more. Wash me clean and make me new. Free me for joyful obedience to you and to live a life that honors you. Help me to love my neighbors. And make me, like John, a witness to your light. In your holy name. Amen.[1]

ACKNOWLEDGMENTS

I'm deeply grateful for the people of The United Methodist Church of the Resurrection for allowing me to serve as their senior pastor. I have shared some of their stories in this book, and there are countless others I did not mention who have inspired me over the years. This book began as an Advent sermon series on John the Baptist that I preached at Church of the Resurrection. I love this congregation that has taught me in so many ways what it means to prepare the way for the Lord in our lives and in our community.

This book would not have been possible without the people at Abingdon Press, led by Susan Salley. I am thankful for her incredible support and collaboration. Thank you, Susan, for all that you do to in support of my books and ministry. I'm also grateful for my editor, Brian Sigmon, whose suggestions, additions, and editorial revisions were valuable as this book took shape. Thank you, Brian! Special thanks also to production manager Tim Cobb for shepherding the book through the production process and overseeing the corrections, images, and illustrations that enrich the book. I'm deeply grateful for the marketing managers, Alan Vermilye and Elizabeth Pruitt, who go above and beyond to help this book and others Abingdon publishes to reach a wide audience. Thank you, Alan and Elizabeth! And thank you to Andrew Weitze, Tracey Craddock, and the many others at Abingdon who worked on this book and accompanying study materials.

I appreciate the whole team at United Methodist Communications, who produce the study videos that accompany this book and enrich the experience of countless individuals and groups through their video ministry. I also want to acknowledge those who develop the leader guides for children, youth, and adults so that congregations can study *Prepare the Way for the Lord* together during Advent. Thank you for the excellent work you've done in preparing these guides.

Finally, I want to thank my best friend and partner of forty years, LaVon Bandy Hamilton. She has supported me and sacrificed in so many ways while I write on nights and weekends. Her love, life, and insights are a constant inspiration to me. She has taught and continues to teach me what it means to prepare the way for the Lord. Thank you, LaVon, for everything. I love you.

NOTES

Introduction

1. I intentionally did not mention which daughter's birth I was describing. The details of their births were slightly different with each, but the preparation and the feelings of anticipation and ultimately overwhelming love were the same with both!

2. "Prayer" in "A Service of Death and Resurrection," *The United Methodist Hymnal* (Nashville: The United Methodist Publishing House, 1989), 871.

3. Sabine MacCormack, "Change and Continuity in Late Antiquity: The Ceremony of *Adventus*." *Historia: Zeitschrift Für Alte Geschichte* 21, no. 4 (1972): 721-52, http://www.jstor.org/stable/4435301.

1. The Annunciation: "God Has Heard Your Prayers"

1. A recent Pew Center survey found 44 percent of adults 18 to 49 who have no children indicated it is not likely that they will have children in the future. Just over half of these said the primary reason is that they simply don't want children.

2. "Infertility," Mayo Clinic, accessed May 2, 2022, https://www.mayoclinic.org/diseases-conditions/infertility/symptoms-causes/syc-20354317.

3. Some scholars believe the last two verses of Malachi were actually added later to be a closing to the entire section of the Prophets in the Tanakh. The Book of Malachi is the final book of the Prophets, but in the Hebrew Bible the order of the sections are the Law, the Prophets, and the Writings, so Malachi is not the last book of the Hebrew Bible, but it is the last book of the Prophets.

4. Susan Silverman, "Havdalah: Taking Leave of Shabbat," My Jewish Learning, accessed May 2, 2022, https://www.myjewishlearning.com/article/havdalah-taking-leave-of-shabbat/.

5. Jackson Donaldson is his name and by now he's in college.

2. Pregnancy, Birth, Circumcision, and Zechariah's Prophecy

1. "Let all Mortal Flesh Keep Silence," Liturgy of St. James, 4th century; trans. by Gerard Moultrie, *The United Methodist Hymnal*, 626.

2. The CEB translates the Hebrew phrase as, "I'm no longer able to have children and my husband's old." The translators here interpret Sarah's pleasure as the joy of having a child. The NRSV maintains the ambiguity of the Hebrew wording.

3. "Video and Full Transcript of George W. Bush's Eulogy for His Father," *New York Times*, December 5, 2018, https://www.nytimes .com/2018/12/05/us/politics/george-w-bush-eulogy.html.

3. John's Ministry and Preaching

1. Notwithstanding the fact that there are some who debate the identification of the Essenes with Qumran, most scholars identify Qumran with the Essenes.

2. At one point Luke tells us that Jesus was "about thirty years old" when he began his public ministry. But if Jesus was only six months younger than John, Jesus would have been about thirty-five when he began his public ministry a few months after John, and thirty-eight when he died, not thirty-three as we usually think. Dates were not exact, but Luke, more than any other Gospel writer, ties events he narrates to specific rulers that can be dated.

4. Witnesses, Testifying to the Light

1. Jim Collins, *Good to Great: Why Some Companies Make the Leap and Others Don't* (New York: HarperCollins, 2001), 22

2. "A Covenant Prayer in the Wesleyan Tradition," John Wesley, *The United Methodist Hymnal*, 607.

3. Josephus, *Antiquities*, 18:116

4. *The United Methodist Hymnal*, 871.

5. The version in *The United Methodist Hymnal*, 400, has "interposed his precious blood." It was changed in the 1980s in some hymnals as people no longer use the word, "interposed."

6. John McCain, "A Light Amid the Darkness," *TIME*, August 18, 2008, 41-42.

Postscript: Judgment Day and the Second Advent

1. Parts of this prayer were adapted from the "Prayer of Confession and Pardon," in the "Service of Word and Table I" of *The United Methodist Hymnal*, 8.

LEARN THE SIGNIFICANCE AND THE POWER OF THE PRAYER JESUS TAUGHT

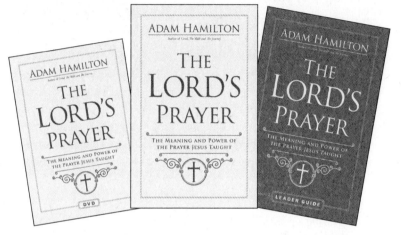

In *The Lord's Prayer: The Meaning and Power of the Prayer Jesus Taught* book and Bible study, best-selling author Adam Hamilton explores each of the prayer's rich lines and examines their meanings in the Bible, illuminating what we ask of God and what we ask of ourselves through its words. Not only will you come to understand its power; you'll learn how to use the Lord's Prayer as a pattern for all of your prayers.

Explore the study at AdamHamilton.com/LordsPrayer.

Watch videos based on
Prepare the Way for the Lord:
Advent and the
Message of John the Baptist
with Adam Hamilton
through Amplify Media.

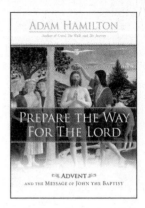

Amplify Media is a multimedia platform that delivers high quality, searchable content with an emphasis on Wesleyan perspectives for churchwide, group, or individual use on any device at any time. In a world of sometimes overwhelming choices, Amplify gives church leaders and congregants media capabilities that are contemporary, relevant, effective, and, most importantly, affordable and sustainable.

With **Amplify Media** church leaders can:

- Provide a reliable source of Christian content through a Wesleyan lens for teaching, training, and inspiration in a customizable library
- Deliver their own preaching and worship content in a way the congregation knows and appreciates
- Build the church's capacity to innovate with engaging content and accessible technology
- Equip the congregation to better understand the Bible and its application
- Deepen discipleship beyond the church walls

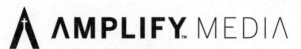

Ask your group leader or pastor about Amplify Media
and sign up today at www.AmplifyMedia.com.